THE LIFE OF A SONG

THE LIFE OF A SONG

The fascinating stories behind
50 of the world's best-loved songs

EDITED BY DAVID CHEAL
AND JAN DALLEY

FINANCIAL
TIMES

BREWER'S

BREWER'S

First published in Great Britain in 2017 by Brewer's, an imprint of Chambers Publishing Limited. An Hachette UK company.

This edition published in 2017 by Chambers Publishing Limited.

Brewer's® is a registered trademark of Chambers Publishing Limited.

British Library Cataloguing in Publication Data:
a catalogue record for this title is available from the British Library.

Library of Congress Catalog Card Number: on file.

ISBN: 978 1 47366 819 5
eISBN: 978 1 47366 818 8

1

The publisher has used its best endeavours to ensure that any website addresses referred to in this book are correct and active at the time of going to press. However, the publisher and the author have no responsibility for the websites and can make no guarantee that a site will remain live or that the content will remain relevant, decent or appropriate.

The publisher has made every effort to mark as such all words which it believes to be trademarks. The publisher should also like to make it clear that the presence of a word in the book, whether marked or unmarked, in no way affects its legal status as a trademark.

Every reasonable effort has been made by the publisher to trace the copyright holders of material in this book. Any errors or omissions should be notified in writing to the publisher, who will endeavour to rectify the situation for any reprints and future editions.

Typeset in Celeste & Anodyne by Palimpsest Book Production Ltd, Falkirk, Stirlingshire
Printed and bound in Great Britain by Clays Ltd, St Ives plc

Chambers Publishing Limited policy is to use papers that are natural, renewable and recyclable products and made from wood grown in sustainable forests. The logging and manufacturing processes are expected to conform to the environmental regulations of the country of origin.

Carmelite House
50 Victoria Embankment
London EC4Y 0DZ
www.chambers.co.uk

CONTENTS

INTRODUCTION

The world's oldest surviving complete song is the 'Seikilos Epitaph'. Around the first century AD, its music and lyrics were engraved in Greek on a tombstone in what is now Turkey. What's remarkable about this song is that a melody written around 2000 years ago still resonates today with anyone familiar with Western music: it's a sweet, sad, memorable tune. The lyrics, meanwhile, are the stuff of songs through the ages: 'Life exists only for a short while/And time demands an end.'

We do not know what instrument it was intended to be played on: perhaps a lyre, or a flute. But, inevitably, it has been picked up and reshaped by modern-day musicians in a panoply of styles: acoustic singer-songwriter, solo harpist, jazz, even dubstep.

This is what happens to good songs: once they've been written and released, they take on a life of their own, reshaped and given new life, often across the generations. And that is what this book is about: a compilation of weekly columns written for *FT Weekend*, it contains the stories of 50 songs that have been born, reborn reinvigorated, re-imagined, and sometimes hideously mangled.

The Life of a Song is not about singers, or stars, or chart success – although of course they come into the story. It is about the music itself. Each of the songs we and the writers have chosen has a rich biography of its own, often transcending and moving between musical genres. Here you will find a song that is now speeding through space, songs that have given rise to court cases, songs that have become funeral favourites, songs that have been used – and abused – by politicians. And every song in this compilation, from pop to jazz, folk, musicals and other genres, has something to say about the human spirit and the experience of being alive that makes them, like the 'Seikilos Epitaph', endlessly young.

David Cheal and Jan Dalley

CONTRIBUTORS

Peter Aspden

Peter Aspden is a former arts editor and writer for the *Financial Times*. He was brought up in Washington DC where he bought his first plastic Beatles wig to sing 'I Want to Hold Your Hand' in front of the mirror. He studied Philosophy, Politics and Economics at St Edmund Hall, Oxford, where he thought that Californian soft rock would change the world. He has written about sport, books, travel and the arts for a wide variety of publications. He is currently thinking about writing a book, but has been sidetracked trying to work out the guitar chords of 'God Only Knows'.

Helen Brown

Helen Brown is an arts journalist whose articles have appeared in the *Financial Times*, the *Daily Telegraph*, the *Independent*, the *Guardian* online, the *New Statesman* and *The Spectator*. Highlights of her interviewing career have included a lesson in playing the guitar with acrylic nails from Dolly Parton, bird-watching with Amy Winehouse and scouring corner shops for fine wines with Grace Jones. She lives in Essex with her two small children and too much vinyl.

David Cheal
David Cheal has been reviewing music since the early 1980s, and was a pop critic for the *Daily Telegraph* for 20 years. He now works on the *Financial Times* arts pages, where he writes and commissions the weekly Life of a Song column and also contributes reviews and features. When he was growing up, he wanted to be Jack Bruce but never got round to learning how to play the bass.

Richard Clayton
After a decade and more of mainly music freelancing for the *Sunday Times* and the *Financial Times*, Richard Clayton swapped tinnitus for timetables to retrain as an English teacher. He remembers interviewing Amy Winehouse over bacon and eggs, and small talk about cycling with Jakob Dylan. Proud to have been an early adopter of Wild Beasts, Kendrick Lamar and Father John Misty, he still hopes to write during the summer holidays.

Mike Hobart
Mike Hobart is the *Financial Times* jazz critic. He was a full-time musician for many years and still plays tenor sax. He now leads his own jazz quintet, whose CD *Evidential* was released last year through anotherworldmusic.

David Honigmann
Building on his misspent youth browsing in Sterns Records, pursuing an interest founded on his parents' copy of 'Missa Luba', David Honigmann is now world music critic for the *Financial Times*. He was also a contributor to the *Rough Guide Book of Playlists*, and is the co-author of a range of children's books. He has only missed one WOMAD this century.

Ludovic Hunter-Tilney

Ludovic Hunter-Tilney is the *Financial Times* pop critic and has also written for the *Guardian*, the *Sunday Times* and the *New Statesman*. In 2014 he won the London Press Club's arts reviewer of the year award. He lives in London.

Hilary Kirby

Hilary Kirby has not yet given up the day job working as an *FT* picture editor, often finding pictures for The Life of a Song column. She loves music, from punk to country, and once (late at night) found her way on to the main stage at Glastonbury. She takes the education of her children's musical taste very seriously and her happiest moments are singing with them to an eclectic range of music in the car.

Ian McCann

Ian McCann is the editor of *Record Collector* magazine, and has written for *NME*, *Q* and the *Independent*, and worked as a reporter on BBC Radio 1. An obsessive accumulator of vinyl, he is a big fan of soul, jazz and reggae, and owns a hi-fi system so loud that it's like the nuclear deterrent: let's hope it will never be used.

Bernadette McNulty

Bernadette McNulty is the deputy arts editor at the *i* newspaper and has written about arts and music for the *Daily Telegraph*, *Financial Times*, *The Observer*, *Harper's Bazaar* and the *Yomiuri Shimbun*. Her ambition growing up was to be a dancer on *Top of the Pops*. She still enjoys interpretive choreography while listening to music in her kitchen.

Charles Morris

Charles Morris was a journalist all his working life, for magazines and then newspapers. He worked for the *Financial Times* for 28 years. From 2006–9 he was the newspaper's sports editor, and specialized in writing about football and tennis. Since retiring in 2014 he has taught journalism at the University of the Arts, London, and been a freelance journalist. He is currently writing a book, a family memoir about football.

Sue Norris

Sue Norris is a former associate editor of the *FT Weekend* magazine and is now a freelance writer and editor. Sue grew up on American soul and funk, and once thought nothing of spending a day's wages on an American import from Contempo Records in London's Hanway Street. She still spends rather too much time watching old episodes of *Soul Train.*

Fiona Sturges

Fiona Sturges is a writer and journalist who specializes in music and popular culture. For 20 years she worked as an interviewer and reviewer for the *Independent*. She is now an arts columnist for the *Financial Times* and the *Guardian*, and lectures in Popular Music Journalism at Southampton Solent University.

Cathi Unsworth

Cathi Unsworth is the author of five pop-cultural crime novels, *Without The Moon, Weirdo, Bad Penny Blues, The Singer* and *The Not Knowing*, all published by Serpent's Tail. She lives in London where she gives regular talks, walks and hosts interviews for The Sohemian Society and Shoreditch House on subjects ranging from true crime, local history, pop art and punk.

MY WAY

'I'd never before written something so chauvinistic, narcissistic, in-your-face and grandiose,' says Paul Anka. But when the former teen idol wrote the lyrics to 'My Way' he was writing for (and in the persona of) his hero Frank Sinatra.

Ol' Blue Eyes was at the end of his (admittedly short) tether in 1967. The Rat Pack was disintegrating, he was being hounded by the FBI over his mob connections, and his 1966 marriage to Mia Farrow was already on the rocks. When a Las Vegas hotel manager cut off his gambling credit (he was heavily in debt to them) Sinatra stormed out, found a golf cart, pushed Farrow into it beside him then drove it through the hotel's front window. The hotel manager punched the caps off the singer's teeth with one clean right hook. The headlines were humiliating.

'Kid, I'm fed up,' 51-year-old Sinatra told 25-year-old Anka. 'I'm gonna do one more album and then I'm out of here. You never wrote me that song you always promised. Don't take too long!'

Anka already owned the rights to a new French song of fading love called 'Comme d'habitude' by Jacques Revaux and singer Claude François (one of France's bestselling singers, until he was electrocuted while straightening a bathroom light fixture in 1978, aged 39). Sleepless in New York, a few months after his dinner with Sinatra, Anka tossed aside François' mournful

lines about a couple who 'make love, as usual/fake it, as usual' and sat down at the piano in search of English lyrics.

'There was a storm brewing,' he recalls, 'and as I played I suddenly sensed myself becoming Frank, tuning into his sense of foreboding. That's how I got the first line: "And now the end is near, and so I face the final curtain." I thought of him leaving the stage, the lights going out, and started typing like a madman, writing it just the way he talked: "Ate it up . . . spit it out." When I finished, it was 5am. I knew Frank was in Las Vegas, but by then he'd be offstage and at the bar. I called: "Frank, I've got something interesting – I'm gonna bring it out." When I played the song for him, he said: "That's kooky, kid. We're going in."'

Sinatra had a minor hit with it in the US on its release in 1969 (where it peaked at Number 27) but it was huge in the UK, where it stayed in the charts for 122 weeks. As it became his signature song Sinatra grew to loathe it, forced to stand before his adoring audience and expose the ugly truth about his aggressive disregard for the thoughts and feelings of other people. 'He was,' says his daughter Tina, 'a man who all his life looked outside for what was missing inside.'

Anka wasn't the only aspiring artist who tried fitting English words to the French song. David Bowie also had a go with 'Even a Fool Learns to Love', later recycling the rejected material as 'Life on Mars?' Hundreds of covers have included a mawkish 1973 version by Elvis (whom Sinatra hated) and a gloriously defiant punk statement by the Sex Pistols' Sid Vicious in 1978. In 2007 Anka (who recorded the song with Jon Bon Jovi) said his favourite covers are by a peppy Nina Simone (1971) and the Gypsy Kings ('A Mi Manera', 1987).

Although it is beloved of karaoke crooners around the world, avoid selecting 'My Way' in the Philippines, where off-key delivery can get you into serious trouble: at least 12 people were shot dead between 2002 and 2012 after altercations over the song.

In 2016 the UK's Co-op funeral company revealed that 'My Way' is now the UK's most popular choice of funeral song, although Sinatra didn't have it played at his own, at which mourners were blasted with a recording of him singing 'Put Your Dreams Away'.

Most recently Nashville-based jazz singer Erin Boheme sang it for Donald and Melania Trump's awkward first dance at his inaugural ball in January 2017. When asked what her dad would think about the 45th president choosing his theme song for the occasion, Nancy Sinatra tweeted: 'Just remember the first line of the song: "And now the end is near".'

Helen Brown

STARMAN

Can a pop song change the world? There are many who claim that when David Bowie performed 'Starman' on the BBC's *Top of the Pops* on 6 July 1972, the earth shifted a little on its axis. Into the dull brown living rooms of Britain was beamed the image of a skinny, slinky young man in a multi-coloured jumpsuit strumming a 12-string acoustic guitar and singing in eccentric vowels about the coming of an alien saviour. And when Bowie draped his arm gently around silver-clad, silver-haired guitarist Mick Ronson's shoulder and pulled him closer to sing the chorus, it's not hard to imagine a nationwide chorus of disapproving harrumphings and newspaper-rattlings. Bowie periodically fixed his eyes on the camera, addressing the viewer directly: 'I had to phone someone so I picked on you-hoo-hoo.' It was electrifying.

Perhaps it's an oversimplification to reduce cultural history to 'moments' but there are certainly plenty of pop stars, fashion designers, artists and writers who claim that Bowie's striking performance was for them a moment of awakening, a realization that they were not alone, that there were others who were 'other'. Among them is Dylan Jones, editor of the UK edition of *GQ* magazine, who has written an entire book (*When Ziggy Played Guitar*) on those fateful few minutes; others include Dave Gahan of Depeche Mode, Marc Almond,

Boy George, Holly Johnson, Ian McCulloch, Gary Numan and Neil Tennant.

But if Bowie was strange, the song was far from it: 'Starman' was an instant pop classic whose glorious chorus echoed the octave-leaping 'Over the Rainbow'. Familiar, too, was the morse-code motif (achieved through a treated synthesis of guitar and piano), signifier of an urgent message and heard earlier on Glen Campbell's 'Wichita Lineman' and on the Supremes' 'You Keep Me Hangin' On' (Vanilla Fudge's version of the same song accentuates this device).

Bowie himself had laboured for three years following his 1969 hit 'Space Oddity' without much success. 'Starman' was his moment; this was his breakthrough.

Over the years various cover versions of 'Starman' have been recorded, few of them noteworthy. One exception came from Brazilian singer Seu Jorge in Wes Anderson's 2004 movie *The Life Aquatic with Steve Zissou*; Jorge's character Pelé dos Santos pops up throughout the film singing Bowie songs in Portuguese, and 'Starman' is beautifully rendered on a warm night with a simple guitar accompaniment and a cigarette. Also, the barmy Finnish band Leningrad Cowboys recorded a memorable cover of the song, all slabby metal guitars and growly vocals (a couple of chords are tweaked to give the song an unsettling edge).

Bowie himself ignored the song for many years but then seemed to fall in love again with his back catalogue in the late 1990s and reintroduced it to his live shows. And his former drummer, Woody Woodmansey, toured with a band that included long-time Bowie producer Tony Visconti, playing Bowie's album *The Man Who Sold the World* in its entirety before cranking out faithfully rendered versions of Bowie hits including 'Starman'.

But this is not the story of how a song has changed and shifted over time. Rather, it's the story of how a song has shifted the times: in popular culture, in fashion, in music, in art. The Victoria and Albert Museum's touring exhibition 'David Bowie Is' featured a massive video wall celebrating Bowie performances, including the *Top of the Pops* performance of 'Starman'. It's a tribute to the song's power that a moment from 1972 has been elevated to the status of art installation.

David Cheal

LIKE A ROLLING STONE

In 2014, the handwritten lyrics to 'Like a Rolling Stone' became the most expensive popular music manuscript to be sold at auction when it fetched just over $2 million at Sotheby's. The lyrics – eventually four verses and a chorus – were based on Dylan's writings on his return from a tour of England in 1965, a vengeful stream of 'vomit' directed at an unknown antagonist, as he later recalled.

When the song was finally released, it changed lives. Bruce Springsteen said the opening snare shot was as if somebody had 'kicked open the door to your mind'. Paul McCartney was almost hypnotized: 'It seemed to go on and on forever. It was just beautiful.' Even Frank Zappa, worldly beyond his years, thought the game was up. 'When I heard "Like a Rolling Stone", I wanted to quit the music business,' he said, 'because I felt "If this wins and it does what it's supposed to do, I don't need to do anything else".'

But the release of Bob Dylan's acerbic single in the summer of 1965 was far from an uncomplicated process. The life of this song began to take shape well before its improbable assault on the charts. It was brought to the songwriter's band during the recording sessions for *Highway 61 Revisited*, the album that would transform Dylan's working methods and status in the popular music pantheon. The release in 2015 of *The Cutting*

Edge 1965–1966, the 12th in Dylan's *Bootleg Series*, reveals the slow metamorphosis of 'Like a Rolling Stone' into the masterpiece it would become. The box set devotes no less than an entire disc to various rehearsals and abandoned versions of the song. It draws vivid portraits of Dylan the experimentalist and Dylan the perfectionist at war with each other as the studio clock ticked away. Here was pop in its most anti-ephemeral form, built to last, as laden with significance as any heftier work of high art.

The song's beginning was inauspicious. Take one is an instrumental run-through in 3/4 time, lurching like a Bavarian drinking song with Dylan's febrile harmonica leading the melody. 'I got lost, man,' says Dylan after one minute. 'Did you get lost?' Pianist Paul Griffin reminds the group of the chord sequence. On take four, Dylan unleashes his vocal for the first time: 'You threw the bums a dime, didn't you?' he sings, and immediately clears his throat, the vehemence of the lyric proving too much for him. 'My voice has gone,' he finally tells the band.

The song is remade, turned into a more orthodox and quicker 4/4 tune, and its first rehearsal sees Dylan's anger muted. His tone is more sardonic, the vocal more reliable. But it lacks the righteous sneer that the devastating lyric demands. And the tempo is too even.

On take four of the remake, serendipity strikes. Session guitarist Al Kooper, 21, a friend of the band, walks in holding his guitar, hoping to join in. He is deemed surplus to requirements, but Dylan decides he wants an organ in addition to the piano, and Kooper volunteers to fill in. He improvises his part, as he would later recall, 'like a little kid fumbling in the dark for a light switch'. And suddenly the song turns into the tumbling, cascading version that will become the finished article.

Dylan is still not happy. He orders 11 more takes of the song, experimenting at one point with a quicker, shuffling tempo, while on another version drummer Bobby Gregg tries some military-style fills. But these remakes are markedly inferior. Dylan and his musicians have already nailed it.

The song was released a month later, at more than six minutes long, much to the disapproval of Columbia Records. What did they know? 'Like a Rolling Stone' reached the Top 10 of most charts, nestling at Number 2 in the US behind The Beatles' 'Help!', another, altogether poppier, cry of existential disarray.

The song has been covered in 50 years' worth of musical styles, and is regularly voted the greatest pop song of all time by those lovingly compiled glossy magazines that wish it was still 1965. Observers have studied the lyrics scribbled in the rare manuscript documents scrupulously to find any hint of the identity of Dylan's victim in the song. All they found were some doodles of a chicken, a hat, and the head of a deer.

Peter Aspden

STAIRWAY TO HEAVEN

In the only memorable moment of the 1992 comedy film *Wayne's World*, the slacker played by Mike Myers visits a guitar shop. He starts to pick out the first four notes of a familiar acoustic arpeggio. Abruptly, the shop owner cuts him off, pointing to a sign that reads 'No Stairway to Heaven'.

The song that became a favourite among budding bedroom guitarists was the highlight of Led Zeppelin's untitled fourth album, and arguably of their entire career. Singer Robert Plant and guitarist Jimmy Page knocked together the outline of the song at a cottage in Wales in 1971 before finishing it off with their bandmates at the Hampshire manor house that was their base for the album.

'Stairway' combines the band's signature themes. It starts with the folksy mysticism with which they had started to experiment on their previous album. The lyrics of 'Stairway' are often taken to be hippie gnosticism, but in fact the opening verse was, in Robert Plant's words, 'about a woman getting everything she wanted all the time without giving back any thought or consideration'.

For the first four minutes of the song, Plant's voice wraps around Jimmy Page's acoustic guitar and multi-tracked recorders played by John Paul Jones. Then, John Bonham's drums reinforce the beat. The tension builds; the tempo subtly accelerates.

A couple of minutes later, Page leans hard into an electric guitar solo and Bonham's drumming suddenly explodes. This is no accident: Bonham was happy with the track he originally laid down, but Page deployed the right mixture of passive-aggression to goad him into another take, on which he audibly sizzles with anger.

'Stairway to Heaven' was never a single – it was too long, and impossible to edit, and in any case the band wanted people to buy the whole album – but it became Led Zeppelin's calling card, regularly performed in concert. 'Does anybody remember laughter?' Plant would enquire rhetorically, mid-verse.

It has, though, had a contested afterlife. Wayne played the riff only in the cinema version of the film because the band, zealously protective at least of their own copyrights, squashed its use in television and home video releases. They were later hit with a lawsuit of their own by the estate of Randy California of the band Spirit, claiming that the opening bore a similarity to his melody for Spirit's song 'Taurus'. In June 2016, after a colourful trial during which Jimmy Page was quizzed as to whether the *Mary Poppins* song 'Chim Chim Cher-ee' might have influenced 'Stairway', a jury in California rejected the claim.

For years after the dissolution of the band in 1980, Plant refused to perform the song, although he was pressed into it for Live Aid (1985), along with Zeppelin colleagues Page and Jones, backed by the drummers of Genesis and Chic, as well as for the 2007 Led Zeppelin reunion that marked the death of their record company boss Ahmet Ertegun. Both renditions were ramshackle. Unlike other Zeppelin warhorses, it is not part of his current set with Plant's band, The Sensational Space Shifters.

But others have attempted it. Frank Zappa and the Mothers went heavy on the prog – it might have been a joke, it might not. Parody band Dread Zeppelin's version sounds like Elvis Presley fronting the Wailers. Lez Zeppelin, an all-woman 'she-incarnation' of the band, played it surprisingly straight.

Among the best covers is Dolly Parton's, which starts with Appalachian guitar and Parton humming the recorder part, and works up into a full-scale hoedown, amid which she sneakily interpolates a couple of extra verses. Rodrigo y Gabriela, amiable Mexican acoustic buskers gone large, remove the words altogether in their Hispanic-flavoured rendition.

In 2012, all three surviving members of Led Zeppelin reunited to be honoured for an evening at the Kennedy Center in Washington DC, with Barack Obama in attendance. Clad in white tie, Plant, Page and Jones saw Ann and Nancy Wilson of Heart perform 'Stairway', accompanied by Bonham's son Jason on drums and by a gospel choir in bowler hats. Page nodded appreciatively to his former comrades. Plant's eyes filled with tears.

David Honigmann

YESTERDAY

In his two performances at the Californian Desert Trip festival in October 2016, Paul McCartney played for nearly three hours each time but still managed to omit one of his most famous songs. 'Yesterday' is one of the most regularly played numbers in the 75-year-old's touring canon, but perhaps he decided that the audience at what was dubbed 'Oldchella' didn't want to be reminded that they were clinging on to the music of the past.

Despite its popularity – it's one of the most covered songs in history – 'Yesterday' has a divisive reputation among listeners: to fans, it's a gorgeously simple, melancholy ballad; to detractors, it's the first major manifestation of McCartney's Achilles heel – his mawkish sentimentality.

Whichever camp you fall into, 'Yesterday' was certainly the seed of future ructions in the band dynamics. McCartney has said that the tune came to him almost fully formed in a dream one night in London in 1963. The then 21-year-old McCartney was living in an attic room in the five-storey Georgian family home in London's Marylebone of his girlfriend, Jane Asher. He had begun dating the 17-year-old after the *Radio Times* sent her to interview The Beatles at a Royal Albert Hall gig earlier that year. The Beatles had just begun renting a flat together on Green Street, just off Park Lane. Despite finally having his own room, McCartney hated the austere surroundings of the sparsely furnished apartment. By contrast, Jane's mother, Margaret Asher, a professor at the Royal Academy of Music, created a warm home for her husband and three children, and invited Jane's boyfriend to come and live with them.

In this cosy atmosphere McCartney woke, he said, with the tune in his head, leapt up, and on the piano next to his bed, hammered out the wistful melody. Convinced that it must be one of the old jazz tunes his father listened to, he played the song to everyone he knew to see if they recognized it.

This was what he was doing one evening at the flat of actress and singer Alma Cogan on Kensington High Street. As he sat playing the still wordless tune to Cogan and her sister Sandra, their mother Fay walked into the living room and asked if anyone would like some scrambled eggs. McCartney sang the words on top of the melody, improvising for the next line: 'Oh baby, how I love your legs.'

'Scrambled eggs' remained the song's lyric until a trip to Portugal in 1965, where McCartney said the words suddenly came to him on the long drive from the airport. He scribbled them down on the back of an envelope. Going into the studio to record the song, the rest of the band found themselves redundant.

George Martin felt that what 'Yesterday' needed was not drums and guitars but a string quartet. McCartney feared that their producer was doing a 'Mantovani' but acquiesced. Because it was a solo performance, and because it was so unlike any of their previous output, The Beatles initially vetoed a release in the UK, letting both Matt Monroe and, ironically, Mantovani have hits with it before they did.

Few of the thousands of covers of the song have enhanced its charms – in the case of Linkin Park's, quite the opposite.

The most fertile period for interpretations was in the five years after it was released, when everyone from Elvis to Frank Sinatra tackled the strange juxtaposition between the chorus and verse.

Most often 'Yesterday' has been like an old mirror, dully reflecting back the style of the singer rather than revealing hidden depths within the song itself. The most successful attempts have tended to be by more singular vocalists, such as Marianne Faithfull's delicate 1965 rendition or Willie Nelson's honeyed drawl on his 1966 live *Country Music Concert* album.

Only Marvin Gaye in 1970 seems to find a whole other 'Yesterday', swapping the plaintive stillness of the original for a swinging soul shuffle and a yearning gospel cry that manages to make being trapped in the past sound almost like heaven rather than hell.

Bernadette McNulty

6

EVERY ROSE
HAS ITS THORN

The record sleeve shows a pensive man with dark stubble, muscular tattooed biceps, a guitar and a cigarette. Confusingly, this otherwise macho rocker also has lustrous blonde hair falling below his shoulders, gold jewellery and voluptuous lips reddened with lipstick. To quote Aerosmith, dude looks like a lady.

He is Poison's singer Bret Michaels, brooding over the break-up that inspired the Los Angeles band's 'Every Rose Has Its Thorn'. Taken from their 1988 album *Open Up and Say . . . Ahh!*, the power ballad was Poison's biggest hit. Number 1 in the US for three weeks, it marked the high-water point of LA's glam metal scene. Dudes who looked like ladies would never rock out with such gusto again.

Glam metal, mocked as 'hair metal', was a pumped-up Reagan-era mutation of 1970s glam rock and punk, headquartered in the fleshpots of West Hollywood's Sunset Strip. Embraced by MTV and fuelled by the decade of excess, it was hugely popular. Poison came late to the scene, since they released their debut album in 1986, but rapidly rose to become one of its biggest names.

'Every Rose Has Its Thorn' was written while they were touring their first album, *Look What the Cat Dragged In*. Late one night after a Dallas show, a homesick Michaels rang his girlfriend, an exotic dancer in LA. The rocker was horrified to hear a male

21

voice answer the phone. 'Now, a female voice, that I could've lived with, you know what I'm saying?' he recalled. 'Hell, I may have even welcomed it! But another guy . . . It broke my heart.' All the pain was poured into 'Every Rose Has Its Thorn'. The song opens with a plaintive sigh and strummed acoustic chords. 'We both lie silently still in the dead of the night,' Michaels sings ponderously. But when guitarist CC DeVille makes a swaggering entrance with a brooding solo, the mood shifts. The drums kick in, the music swells up and Michaels' voice acquires a certain lip-smacking relish for the infidelity he is supposedly lamenting.

Lyrical juxtapositions recur. Roses have thorns, nights have dawns, a couple lie close but 'feel miles apart inside'. To have this sung by a man in lipstick and make-up adds a weird gravity to Michaels' doggerel.

Somewhere in the depths of 'Every Rose Has Its Thorn' lie Shakespeare's sonnets. Number 35, to be precise – the one in which the poet forgives the 'master-mistress of my passion' for a 'trespass' against his love. 'No more be grieved at that which thou hast done', he tells the androgynous youth. 'Roses have thorns . . .'

'Every Rose Has Its Thorn' was LA glam metal's most abiding memento, its 'Stairway to Heaven' – an association suggested by the 1991 film *Bill & Ted's Bogus Journey* in which the bodacious duo Bill and Ted are confronted by St Peter at the gates of heaven asking, 'What is the meaning of life?' They respond by reciting lines from 'Every Rose Has Its Thorn'.

That was the start of the song's fruitful afterlife. It is a film and television soundtrack staple, from *Glee* to *The Simpsons*, has been belted out by contestants on *American Idol* and no doubt is being slaughtered right now by a karaoke caterwauler. Miley Cyrus reinterpreted it as a big pop number in 2009.

The shameless Michaels – who went on to star in a reality television show, *Rock of Love*, in which women competed to be his girlfriend – remakes it at regular intervals, including a kids' version sung by his young daughters and a seniors' version with country veteran Loretta Lynn.

The shape-shifting is apt. Poison's mighty power ballad marks the last popular flourish of transvestism in rock, a tradition stretching back from the New York Dolls to David Bowie and Mick Jagger. Since LA glam metal was consigned to history by grunge, its scruffy Pacific Coast nemesis, male rockers have adopted a duller mode of dress. The days of stubble and lip gloss are over. 'Every Rose Has Its Thorn' is a break-up song in more ways than one.

Ludovic Hunter-Tilney

SURF'S UP

If there is one song that encapsulates the psychologically disturbed brilliance of Brian Wilson at his creative peak, it is 'Surf's Up'. He wrote it in 1966 while sitting at the piano at home in California in his 'sandpit' – he liked to feel the sand between his toes – at a time when he was deteriorating mentally. He was suffering symptoms of what would eventually be diagnosed as bipolar schizoaffective disorder, as well as embarking on a long period of drug abuse. The song took about half an hour to write.

'Surf's Up' first surfaced in a 1967 CBS television special, *Inside Pop: The Rock Revolution*, presented by Leonard Bernstein, with Wilson singing it solo at the piano. But then the song disappeared and began to acquire a special mystique. The album for which it was intended, *Smile*, remained unfinished for decades. In the CBS film, Bernstein said he was 'fascinated by the strange and compelling scene called "pop music"', and rightly so: this was a period when pop was beginning to take itself seriously, pushing boundaries. In 1965 The Beatles had released their ground-breaking *Rubber Soul* album, launching a transatlantic to-and-fro with The Beach Boys, who responded with *Pet Sounds*, which in turn was released around the same time as The Beatles' *Revolver*.

But then Wilson became mired in the quicksand of *Smile*.

Part of the problem with the album was Wilson's decision to ditch fellow Beach Boy Mike Love as lyricist and hire the young composer, arranger and lyricist Van Dyke Parks. Parks' lyrics for *Smile* were dazzling but often so impressionistic as to be almost abstract, and Love made his feelings clear about what he called, derisively, Parks' 'acid alliteration'. Alongside fractious studio sessions, Wilson was under pressure from the record company, Capitol, to write more hits. He began to descend further into isolation. By May 1967 *Smile* had been abandoned. On 1 June *Sgt Pepper* was released. Game over.

In 1971 The Beach Boys finally released 'Surf's Up' on an album of the same name. Fleshed out with a band, brass and harmonies, the song was beguiling and enigmatic: another 'pocket symphony' to follow 1966's revolutionary 'Good Vibrations'. Wilson, of course, never actually surfed. Parks' lyric was catching a different kind of wave, the emerging 1960s counterculture, the rise of the baby boomers, and the phrase 'surf's up' arrives at a point in the song where it is marking a transition from old to new, from age to youth: 'Surf's Up/Aboard a tidal wave/Come about hard and join/The young and often spring you gave'. Later, the lyric echoes William Wordsworth: 'The child is father of the man.'

Wilson went on to spend decades in the wilderness, but in 2002 he was well enough to launch a tour of the UK on which he performed, in its entirety, *Pet Sounds*. With his crack ensemble of players and singers, he then went back into the studio to complete *Smile*, which was released in 2004. As an album, *Smile* doesn't quite hold together; it's no *Sgt Pepper*. But 'Surf's Up' is easily its finest moment, a little masterpiece of shifting keys and tempi, and it's no surprise that few have attempted to cover it. There's a hypnotically strange, woozy

2001 rendition by art-punk singer David Thomas and Two Pale Boys. Jimmy Webb, David Crosby and Vince Gill sang it faithfully at a 2001 'All Star Tribute to Brian Wilson' in New York. But that's about it.

Discussions about the finest version, therefore, centre on the recordings made by Wilson and The Beach Boys, of which there are many: three alone on *The Smile Sessions* box set (released in 2011). One such features Wilson alone at his piano in 1967. Listen to his left hand; he seems to make the notes bend. And listen to the voice, both fragile and pure. It's exquisite.

David Cheal

MIDNIGHT TRAIN TO GEORGIA

The great American soul band Gladys Knight & The Pips had one of their biggest hits in 1973 with the heartbreak narrative of big-city failure in 'Midnight Train to Georgia'. The much-covered soul classic tells the story of a woman whose man once dreamed of superstardom in LA but, his hopes crushed, is retreating to – as the song puts it – 'a simpler place and time'. The female narrator is declaring that her place is alongside him: 'I'd rather live with him in his world/Than live without him in mine'.

The tune joined a rich body of American, especially African–American, train songs in the US, stretching from the Delta blues to R&B, although this is a song of retreat rather than escape. Yet when singer-songwriter Jim Weatherly wrote it as a pop-country number in 1972, he was thinking not of trains or even of Georgia, but of a throwaway line from his former foot-ball buddy Lee Major's girlfriend, Farrah Fawcett. Chatting on the phone to Weatherly, Fawcett – soon to be a superstar herself in *The Six Million Dollar Man* and *Charlie's Angels* – said she was packing to catch a midnight plane to Houston. The line teased away at Weatherly, and 'Midnight Plane to Houston' was the title he gave the song that he recorded himself soon after writing it, in which it is the man who faithfully upends his life for a woman.

The soul singer Cissy Houston (mother of Whitney) heard 'Midnight Plane to Houston' and decided to record its first cover version, in January 1973. But the title irked. It wasn't the collision of Houstons – singer and subject – that bothered her, but one of authenticity. If she was going to sing this song, she had to feel it. And, she later said, 'My people are originally from Georgia and they didn't take planes to Houston or anywhere else. They took trains.'

Cissy's producer asked Weatherly for permission to change the title and lyrics to reflect that. 'We said, "Change anything but the writer and publisher",' the songwriter told Gary James of the Classic Bands website. 'Midnight Train to Georgia' was the title that stuck, even when Weatherly re-recorded his own song in 2003.

Cissy Houston had a respectable R&B hit with her account of the song, giving it a female voice and, by adding harmonica, a country-ish feel. It was this version that Gladys Knight was to hear soon afterwards. Gladys Knight & The Pips had already had a hit with another Jim Weatherly song, 'Neither One of Us (Wants to Be the First to Say Goodbye)', in 1972. They recorded the renamed 'Midnight Train' in August 1973. They too added to and tweaked some of the lines, again with Weatherly's blessing. It was Knight who upgraded the man's longing for success in Los Angeles to an ambition to be a superstar. Knight's version is also wordier than both previous recordings, to take account of the important vocal role played by the Pips.

The song went on to hit Number 1 and to win a Grammy. But, as with the similarly travel-themed Glen Campbell song, 'By the Time I Get to Phoenix', some listeners challenged its logistics. Geoff Turner, a producer at Canada's CBC Radio and 'son of a rail nut', only recently confirmed with Amtrak that there were no trains from LA leaving for Georgia at midnight in August 1973, or indeed any direct trains. In 2016 he got in touch with Weatherly about the apparent error, who explained the evolution of the title to him. 'So many little miracles . . . happened to make that song get to where it got, in Gladys's hands,' said Weatherly. 'It was just totally amazing to me.'

Over the years Weatherly will have been grateful he insisted on his copyright, as covers emerged from performers as diverse as Aretha Franklin, Neil Diamond, Garth Brooks (who used the third person) and the comedian Sandra Bernhard.

Gladys Knight's version of the song is beautifully embellished by her backing singers, The Pips, with their signature lines and railroad 'Whoo-whoos'. And in 1977 they had their moment in the spotlight on a Richard Pryor television special. Contractual

difficulties had forced the band apart temporarily, so the Pips (billed, literally, as 'And the Pips') performed their entire backing vocals to 'Midnight Train' – alongside a spot-lit lone mic stand where Gladys Knight should have been. It was a triumph.

Sue Norris

LADY
MARMALADE

It was seen as the height of sophistication in the disco era to include a little French in your lyrics; after all, 'discotheque' is French for 'record library'. Grace Jones covered Edith Piaf's 'La Vie en Rose'. Chic chanted 'Le Freak' and produced French pop plodders Sheila & B Devotion, with Sheila's Gallic accent to the fore. However, the francophone floor-filling trend was started by a veteran Philadelphia soul trio, Labelle, and their break-through 'Lady Marmalade' revealed the advantages of singing *en français*: many listeners and broadcasters didn't realize how provocative the song was.

Unfortunately, neither did the group's lead singer.

'Lady Marmalade' had been dreamt up by Bob Crewe, a human hit machine whose credits included The Four Seasons' 'Rag Doll' and The Walker Brothers' 'The Sun Ain't Gonna Shine Anymore'. One of Crewe's projects was a group called The Eleventh Hour, fronted by singer Kenny Nolan. In 1974 the pair wrote a gritty song called 'Lady Marmalade', its prowling groove reflecting a sleazy lyric. Crewe's Lady Marmalade was a Creole sex worker in New Orleans, approaching men with the sassy line, 'Voulez-vous coucher avec moi, ce soir?' He supposedly heard the phrase on the lips of hookers while visiting the French Quarter, although more likely he remembered Blanche DuBois purring it in Tennessee Williams' *A Streetcar Named Desire*.

The Eleventh Hour's version didn't sell, so Crewe pitched it to Patti LaBelle. She told him: 'I don't know what that *voulez-vous* stuff means . . . but that's a hit.' Her group needed one: Labelle had been around for a decade in various guises, and despite the patronage of Dusty Springfield, the Rolling Stones and the young Elton John in the 1960s, stardom remained elusive. In 1974, armed with Crewe and Nolan's song, Labelle flew south to work with Allen Toussaint, the linchpin of the New Orleans studio scene throughout the 1960s and 1970s. He shredded 'Lady Marmalade', placing the streetwalker at the heart of the tale rather than objectifying her. The cream of New Orleans' soul musicians played on the session, including three-quarters of The Meters, articled funk legends. The result was a deeply funky tune dressed in disco glitter, and Labelle sang it like an empowering anthem. It went to Number 1 in the US. Some critics assumed Toussaint had written it, a myth repeated in some of his obituaries when he died in 2015, but he composed little of *Nightbirds*, the album it graced.

The seductive nature of the song meant it was never short of cover-version customers. Québécoise singer Nanette Workman went the whole hog by singing it entirely in French in 1975. That year Latin bandleader Mongo Santamaria's brassy instrumental interpretation sounded like a theme for a TV cop show. A former percussionist with Prince, SheilaE, gave 'Marmalade' a highly arranged R&B twist in 1991. Although Labelle's single didn't hit Number 1 in the UK, All Saints rectified that in 1997, the female quartet singing it like a cross between Bananarama and Destiny's Child in a sanded-down cover, complete with cheesy rap.

The Camembert content climaxed with Christina Aguilera, Lil' Kim, Mya and Pink's update in 2001 for the soundtrack of

the movie *Moulin Rouge*, making it the only song to top the charts twice in the US and the UK. With each subsequent version, the 'sexiness' grew more overstated and the empowerment factor fell.

Patti LaBelle claimed she hadn't understood the French come-on in 'Lady Marmalade' at first. She told *Jet* magazine: 'Nobody told me what I'd just sung about.' When she found out, she felt 'I'd turned into some kind of bad girl'. Ironically, it wasn't even the rudest song on *Nightbirds*. That dubious honour went to 'You Turn Me On', which details female pleasure in graphic terms. Perhaps Ms LaBelle didn't understand that, either.

Ian McCann

GOD BLESS
THE CHILD

For a song that has become something of a secular hymn, it's strange that Billie Holiday's plaintive 'God Bless the Child' grew out of a row with her mother. But then, as Tony Bennett said of Holiday: 'When you listen to her, it's almost like an audio tape of her autobiography. She didn't sing anything unless she lived it.'

'God Bless the Child' is attributed to both Holiday and Arthur Herzog Jnr, although both later claimed sole credit for it. The song was hastily written in 1939, and Holiday said she wrote it in a rage after her mother refused to give her a small loan – at a time when Holiday was bankrolling her restaurant. 'She wouldn't give me a cent. I was mad at her, she was mad at me . . . Then I said, "God bless the child that's got his own", and walked out', according to her autobiography *Lady Sings the Blues*. The vocalist stewed for three weeks before 'a whole damn song' fell into place and she rushed to Greenwich Village to ask songwriter Herzog to help sort the tune out. 'We changed the lyrics in a couple of spots, but not much,' she wrote.

But Herzog tells a different tale, according to Donald Clarke's biography of Holiday. Here, the still-angry singer told Herzog about the argument, and got to the part when she stormed off with the words 'God bless the child'. Herzog interrupted with 'What's that mean?' Twenty minutes later, they had a song.

According to Herzog, Holiday's only contribution, apart from the title and story, was to take one note down by a half step. Herzog found a publisher the next day, although Holiday did not record it until 1941, for the Okeh label with the Eddie Haywood Orchestra. It was a moderate hit, peaking at Number 25 in the Billboard charts. The lyrics interweave the original spat into seeming folk-mottos and biblical references. The opening lines, 'Them that's got shall have/Them that's not shall lose/So the Bible says, and it still is news', echo St Matthew's parable of the talents: 'For to all those who have, more will be given . . .'.

But as the song progresses, the lyrics shift the parable – man's duty to make the most of what you have been given – into a different context. The line 'Rich relations give crusts of bread and such, you can help yourself, but don't take too much' captures survival in an unequal world.

Holiday returned to the song several times before she died aged 44 in 1959, including with the Count Basie band in 1952 – a video clip shows her in front of the slowly swaying brass section. She sang it differently every time, altering phrasing, placement and pitch, yet creating in the listener the illusion that they were hearing each note exactly as originally written.

Jazz instrumentalists later developed the song, though it took more than a decade for the song to resurface. Sonny Rollins recorded it first as an epic ballad on the 1962 album *The Bridge*, and later as a soulful canter over the new rhythms of funk on the 1973 album *Horn Culture*. Eric Dolphy's rippling unaccompanied reading on the 1963 Illinois Concert confirmed the bass clarinet as a jazz instrument. A sombre, soulful and brassy vocal cover was a Top 10 hit for the jazz-rock band Blood Sweat and Tears in 1969.

The best-known vocal versions tend to be from singers paying homage to Holiday. Diana Ross launched her film career capturing some of Holiday's fragile strength in the 1972 biopic *Lady Sings the Blues*, and Tony Bennett duetted with the digital ghost of Holiday on the track for his 1997 tribute album *Tony Bennett on Holiday*. José James last year recorded a prowling blues-laced version on his Holiday songbook album *Yesterday I Have the Blues*.

The song was part of the soundtrack in Steven Spielberg's 1993 film *Schindler's List* – jazz was banned under the Nazis, so the scene emphasized Schindler's renunciation of the regime. Even *The Simpsons* slipped in some reverence on their 1990 *The Simpsons Sing the Blues* album, with a version that includes some tasty sax from Bleeding Gums Murphy, after Lisa Simpson demands a live band. The Moby and Oscar the Punk electronica remix was a mistake.

The song's title has even been pulled into service in an education debate in the US about the role of charter schools. It turns up at funerals and birth celebrations alike. Like the parable, the song has prompted many interpretations.

Mike Hobart

IN THE AIR
TONIGHT

The coolification of Phil Collins is among pop's most curious turn-arounds. The former Genesis drummer and frontman scored seven Number 1 singles in the US, and more than 100 million album sales worldwide, after launching his career as a solo singer in 1981 with 'In the Air Tonight'. By the mid-1990s, though, his name was mud with critics, and as popular tastes changed, his earnest balladry came to be seen as corny as one of his flat caps.

That today he is lauded by Lorde, the influential New Zealand singer-songwriter, covered by Kanye West and remotely fist-bumped by Brooklyn hipsters such as Yeasayer is largely down to gangsta rap, a Cadbury's chocolate-promoting gorilla and the 'gated reverb' drum sound of 'In the Air Tonight'.

Hip-hop never got the memo about Collins being uncool. 'Don't mess with my Phil,' Ice-T (of 'Cop Killer' fame) reportedly once told a disparaging hack. DMX sampled the eerie synth line and core lyric of 'In the Air Tonight' on 'I Can Feel It' in 1998. What he, and others including Nas and Tupac, heard in that song is probably the same emotional directness and atmospheric production that make it an obvious template for the current wave of murky, downtempo R&B, exemplified by acts from James Blake to The Weeknd. Built around the ominous chant, 'I can feel it coming in the air tonight, oh Lord', you might well call Collins's track, the opener of his 1981 debut solo album *Face Value*, ambient blues.

Having played with Brian Eno in the 1970s, Collins understood ambient music. He wrote the song at the lowest of ebbs and in the saddest of keys, D minor. His first wife had left him, so he set up a studio in his bedroom and poured out his pain over a Prophet-5 synthesizer and a Roland CR-78 drum machine. The words were mostly improvised. Collins continues to maintain he doesn't know what the song means beyond it being a litany of 'anger, bitterness and hurt'.

It took Ahmet Ertegun, the boss of Atlantic, to encourage him to turn the demo into a proper record, and the rest is Collins's solo career. The characteristic drum sound – which became a blueprint for much 1980s rock and funk – was a happy accident. It had been discovered by Collins and the engineer Hugh Padgham when the pair were working on Peter Gabriel's third album. By chance, Padgham heard Collins's drums in the studio through the 'talkback' microphone on a new console; with the room echo, they sounded huge and wonderfully distorted.

Padgham added a 'noise gate' effect to increase the punchiness of the signal by cutting it off quickly: the sonic equivalent of not knowing what has hit you. With Padgham then producing the album *Face Value*, they recreated the technique to produce one of the most celebrated drum breaks on 'In the Air Tonight'.

The way the drums batter out of the album version is like a defiant snarl of rage, all the more powerful and surprising for the minimal build-up. For the single, Ertegun insisted an initial backbeat be overdubbed for easier listening. The song was only pipped as a UK Number 1 by John Lennon's posthumous chart-topper 'Woman'.

But the advertising agency behind a famous British 2007 chocolate bar television commercial shrewdly used the original. The drumming gorilla seems to have been waiting all his life before launching into his big fill (pun intended).

Aged 66, Collins is now capitalizing on his newfound credibility by reissuing his catalogue under the rubric *Take a Look at Me Now*. Not everyone is pleased that he is 'no longer in retirement'. Thousands of people have signed a jocular petition to 'stop' him returning to music. It would be churlish of even the most pernickety troll to deny that 'In the Air Tonight' still raises the nape hairs, 36 years on.

Richard Clayton

12

AMSTERDAM

Jacques Brel was born into a bourgeois Belgian family in 1929, but as he grew up he came to loathe what he called the 'mediocrity of the spirit' that infected his comfortable world. The songs that he went on to write when he moved to Paris and became one of the world's foremost French-language singers and songwriters were the work of a man of many passions.

One of his most torrid songs was 'Amsterdam', and the song's birth testified to its emotional power. His publicist and mistress Sylvie Rivet later recalled that she and Brel were in the south of France in 1964. 'One morning at six o'clock Brel read the words of "Amsterdam" to Fernand, a restaurateur who was about to set off fishing for ingredients for a bouillabaisse. Overcome, Fernand broke out in sobs and cut open some sea urchins to help control his emotion.'

Brel's 'Amsterdam' vividly portrays the lives of the sailors, drunks and whores of the port of Amsterdam, its 3/4 time signature evoking their dance steps; when he first sang it on stage at Paris's Olympia in 1964, the crowd gave him a three-minute ovation. Footage of Brel's performances of 'Amsterdam' shows him twitching, jerking and pouring sweat as the song's feverish crescendo reaches its peak: then, blackout. Three minutes of pure drama.

Inevitably, 'Amsterdam' was translated into English, and here

Brel had two champions: Rod McKuen and Mort Shuman. McKuen was a singer, songwriter and poet whose translations of two Brel songs became pop hits: 'Ne Me Quitte Pas' became the widely covered 'If You Go Away'; 'Le Moribund' became the schmaltzy 'Seasons in the Sun', a hit for Terry Jacks in 1974. McKuen's 'Amsterdam' took many poetic liberties with Brel's lyric but was not widely adopted.

Meanwhile Shuman, American singer and songwriter, also took up the Brel banner. His translated lyrics to many Brel songs, including 'Amsterdam', have become the 'standard' versions, retaining Brel's spirit, although with perhaps less of his poetic abstraction. Shuman also paid tribute to Brel by co-writing a 1968 off-Broadway show, *Jacques Brel Is Alive and Well and Living in Paris*, which became a 1975 film. (In the film Shuman sings 'Amsterdam' in a bar while Brel himself sits silently in a corner, nursing a Stella Artois.)

One singer who was drawn to Brel via Shuman was Scott Walker. As one half of The Walker Brothers, Walker had had hits with pop tunes such as 'The Sun Ain't Gonna Shine Any More' but by 1967 he was showing an appetite for the fringes of popular music (an appetite that would culminate in his 2006 album *The Drift*, on which a percussionist was required to slap a piece of raw pork). Walker covered a string of Brel songs in the 1960s, among them 'Amsterdam' (they would eventually be collected on the fabulous 1981 album, *Scott Walker Sings Jacques Brel*). Walker's 'Amsterdam' follows the Brel–Shuman template, its big arrangement and potent lyrics summoning up a scene of tragic debauchery.

Then there was David Bowie. As early as 1969, Bowie was covering Brel songs (again, in Shuman's translations): he sang 'My Death' at the Beckenham Arts Lab that year, and again at

his 'farewell Ziggy' concerts in London in 1973. Later in 1973 when he released the single 'Sorrow', 'Amsterdam' was the B-side. Bowie's version is stripped down, with only an acoustic guitar for accompaniment, but is no less dramatic for that: 'And he pisses like I cry' is delivered with spine-tingling intensity. A new generation had been brought to Brel.

Subsequent versions by Irish singer Camille O'Sullivan (who gives the song a cabaret vibe) and folk band Bellowhead (ramshackle and rowdy) have brought the song to a wider audience. And in 2003 it was performed in the unlikely environment of the French TV talent show *À la Recherche de la Nouvelle Star* when a young singer, Thierry Amiel, sang it to a studio of swaying, banner-waving supporters. The show may have been cheesy, but Amiel nailed the song (although he came second in the contest). Over the years, the song has attracted a particular kind of singer, drawn to its swirling maelstrom of emotions – artists for whom, like Brel, mediocrity is anathema.

David Cheal

13

WITHOUT YOU

In December 1969, an unknown band called Badfinger released 'Come and Get It', a catchy pop song written by Paul McCartney, who had given it to the band to help them break into the charts. It worked. But it was the wrong song for the wrong band at the wrong time. Watch their performance on the BBC's *Top of the Pops*: the group – earnest and long-haired – seem almost embarrassed by the song's primary-coloured glibness. This was the end of the 1960s. Music was getting darker, more complicated. Surely they could do better than that.

While McCartney's ditty was giving them instant chart recognition, two of the group's members, Pete Ham and Tom Evans, were hatching a more dramatic song back in their Golders Green bedsits. 'Without You' was written about the two men's relationships with their girlfriends: Ham wrote the verse, Evans the chorus. The song was full of epic observations on the fragility of love.

'No I can't forget tomorrow/When I think of all my sorrow/When I had you there/But then I let you go,' wrote Ham of his romantic entanglement; 'I can't live, if living is without you,' said Evans of his own. The band performed the song with little sense of conviction or self-belief. It was buried, along with its tired, plodding arrangement, on the end of side one of their 1970 album *No Dice*.

46

Harry Nilsson was an American singer-songwriter who was famous for a song he didn't write: the lovely 'Everybody's Talkin', Fred Neil's get-away-from-it-all folk tune, which became the theme of the 1969 film *Midnight Cowboy*. Now, at a party, he heard Badfinger's 'Without You', another song with potential (legend has it that he thought it was written by The Beatles: easy to believe).

Nilsson got together with American producer Richard Perry and they transformed the song, which was a hit in early 1972. A two-note piano intro leads into Nilsson's tender, high vocal. The fragility of love is given its appropriate arrangement. An orchestral backing is subtly hued, and the slide into the chorus tastefully negotiated.

But then, on the first repetition of 'I can't live, if living is without you', Nilsson lets himself go. It is the moment when resignation turns into something hotter and wilder. 'I can't give, I can't give any more,' Nilsson sings, desperately, and you cannot but believe him. He turns the delicate song into what would later be known as a power ballad; except that he himself is powerless, vanquished by his dependency.

The song was a massive hit all over the world. It became a standard, recorded by some 180 artists and, of course a karaoke favourite, if you were really far gone. And then, in 1994, it emerged again, this time from the formidable vocal cords of Mariah Carey.

Her version is smooth, polished, breathy, crowded with melismatic flourishes. It is everything that continues to be wrong with popular balladry today. The fragility is gone, the tentativeness nowhere to be found. On a video of a live performance, you can hear the audience revving up during each crescendo of the chorus. 'I can't live,' sings Carey, but she is only girding

herself for greater glory. At the end of the song, a gospel choir joins in: of course it does. 'No, I can't live, No I can't live.' The song, released the week after Nilsson's death from a heart attack at the age of 52, was a huge success.

What is it like to feel like you can't live? The song's writers, Pete Ham and Tom Evans, both knew. They hanged themselves, in separate incidents, Ham in 1975, Evans in 1983. Among their concerns had been ongoing rows about royalties from 'Without You'. People talked of the 'curse' of Badfinger. The band that wanted to get away from simple pop songs, and delve into the darker waters of human despair.

Peter Aspden

IT'S THE HARD KNOCK LIFE

Listen a lot to Katy Perry's 'Roar' (yes, I have two daughters) and you will notice the outline of another song within the 2013 mega-hit. It's there in the jabbing piano chords at the beginning and the jaunty beat that tells us that, although poor Katy has been dealt a harsh hand by love, the plucky gal is going to be just fine.

The song being echoed is that great anthem of American resilience 'It's the Hard Knock Life', from the 1977 Broadway musical *Annie*. It is sung by the inmates of the girls' orphanage where the eponymous heroine is incarcerated, a grim brick pile in Depression-era New York. There, we encounter an unmitigated picture of hardship, a 'full of sorrow life' without kisses or treats, a place where, as 'It's the Hard Knock Life' dolefully informs us, Santa Claus never treads. It's a scenario straight from the blues. 'Once a day don't you wanna throw the towel in?' the girls chorus. Yet they deliver their lament in indomitably chirpy all-American voices, bulwarked by that jaunty beat that later turns up in 'Roar'.

Meanwhile (in the wonderful 1982 film) the drudgery of cleaning the orphanage is transformed into cheery dance routines with mops and brushes. At the end of the song, rather than throw in the towel, Annie attempts a bold escape in a trolley of dirty laundry. She ain't a quitter. 'It's the Hard Knock

Life' was ingeniously revived by Jay-Z on his 1998 track 'Hard Knock Life (Ghetto Anthem)', adopting the girls' perky chorus as an accompaniment to his rags-to-riches tales of Brooklyn hustling, with the song's beat recast as hip-hop. It was a world-wide hit, the song, like Annie's laundry basket, that smuggled him into the mainstream.

Jay-Z gained permission to use the 'Hard Knock Life' sample by writing a letter to the musical's composer Charles Strouse and lyricist Martin Charnin expounding on his childhood love of the show, having won a ticket to see it on Broadway as a prize in an essay-writing competition at his hard-knock Bedford-Stuyvesant school. The letter was, he later admitted, an 'exaggeration'. In fact the rapper came across the hip-hop version, by producer Mark 'the 45 King' James, at a rap show and bought it for a rumoured $10,000.

His association with *Annie* continues with the recent film remake. Co-produced by the rapper, it updates the story to present-day New York and gives the soundtrack a hip-hop makeover. The result was roasted by the critics. Yet 'It's the Hard Knock Life' has all the bustling energy of old, neatly prefaced by one of the foster girls (orphanages are so 1930s) asking what a 'hard knock life' means. 'It means our life sucks!' spits a colleague.

Katy Perry pops up in the new *Annie*, tweeting about her love for the heroine. In 'Roar', 'It's the Hard Knock Life' leads a medley of empowerment references. Helen Reddy's feminist anthem 'I Am Woman' (1972) is alluded to in the title ('I am woman, hear me roar'). Survivor's *Rocky* theme tune 'Eye of the Tiger' is quoted in the lyrics. The context is Perry's divorce from comedian Russell Brand. Co-written with her friend, singer-songwriter Bonnie McKee, 'Roar' gives a Californian spin to Annie's tale of hard-won social mobility. Perry celebrates going 'from zero to my own hero', a dazzling act of personal validation. It's like orphan Annie graduating from the school of hard knocks, moving to LA and swapping Sandy the dog for a personal trainer. You go, girl.

Ludovic Hunter-Tilney

15

APACHE

What links Burt Lancaster and the birth of hip-hop? Or pioneer rappers the Sugarhill Gang and the B-movie *The Thing with Two Heads*? Or a Danish Eurovision winner and a Native American rebel? The answer is a tale as wild and random as the best kind of party night, and it revolves around the Incredible Bongo Band's reworking of 'Apache', once described as 'the most crazed piece of orchestral funk ever recorded'.

The story begins in 1959 when the English songwriter Jerry Lordan was inspired by the Robert Aldrich film *Apache*. It starred Lancaster as a brave holding out as Geronimo surrendered. Lordan wrote a stirring instrumental that he sold to the guitar whizz Bert Weedon, the man behind the 1957 book *Play in a Day* that taught generations of famous names – Paul McCartney, Eric Clapton and Brian May among them. Weedon cut a version, but his record company sat on it. Frustrated, Lordan passed the music on to The Shadows, and their dramatic, hard-riding rendition – released in July 1960, with Hank Marvin's twangy guitar to the fore – became an unexpected UK Number 1. Weedon's slower, almost wistful 'Apache' snuck out the next month. It only made Number 24.

February of the following year saw Jorgen Ingmann, future Eurovision winner, take his cover to Number 2 in the US. Twinkly, even slightly prissy, it nevertheless ensured that 'Apache' was already something like a phenomenon. Later in 1961, the country singer Sonny James did a vocal version. 'Alone, all alone by the campfire/She dreamed of her love,' he croons. Cheesy, but curiously affecting, his ballad is just waiting for Quentin Tarantino to rediscover it. There were three other guitar versions of note in the 1960s – by the surf-rocky Ventures, the fuzzier Davie Allan and The Arrows, and those bad-acid growlers the Edgar Broughton Band.

By the 'Flower Power' era, however, 'Apache' was redolent of a squarer time. It needed a Hollywood makeover to become a dance floor smash and one of the most sampled tunes in history: enter MGM's soundtracks director Michael Viner and *The Thing with Two Heads*. Viner was given the job of providing incidental music for that shlocky 1972 flick. One of his numbers, 'Bongo Rock', caught on enough that he reconvened the session musicians who had made it to record an album of the same name. This group, which included the Motown conga player King Errisson and the Pet Sounds and Derek and the Dominoes drummer Jim Gordon, was hastily dubbed the Incredible Bongo Band. Track two on their soon-to-be-obscure 1973 LP was an infectiously percussive, horn-fuelled and organ-driven 'Apache'.

It came to the attention of a Bronx DJ, a Jamaican known as Kool Herc. He claims the credit for extending the percussion break on 'Apache' together with similar tracks or a copy of the same record. His so-called 'Merry-Go-Round' sent clubbers 'hype'. By the end of the 1970s, such 'breakbeats' had emerged as the cornerstone of hip-hop – as joyously confirmed by the Sugarhill Gang's 1981 'Apache', complete with exhortations for Tonto and Kemo-Sabe to 'jump on it'.

The Incredible Bongo Band broke up in 1974 – King Errisson

later touring with Neil Diamond, and Michael Viner becoming a publisher who died of cancer in 2009. Jim Gordon, who suffers from schizophrenia, remains in prison for murdering his mother in 1983.

Their break has been looped and chopped, spliced and diced, repackaged and repurposed, by artists from LL Cool J to Missy Elliott, and Moby to Goldie. For an exhaustive list, look up the blogger Michaelangelo Matos. (He deserves an award for services to musical genealogy.) There's also an entire documentary about it, *Sample This* (2012). But if all that's starting to seem a bit po-faced, check out the Tommy Seebach Band's ineffably camp 1977 disco-rock 'Apache': it's hard to believe it's not some stupendous mickey-take. All the same, you'll want to dance.

Richard Clayton

16

1999

The year was 1982 and an androgynous young man named Prince had become a familiar presence on the radio and in the charts. But this was the year when he was to become a household name. From the beginning a prodigious recording artist, the mononymous Minneapolitan had released four albums in three years; his fifth was to be his breakthrough, its title track, '1999', a bracing blast of funk.

The album was the first to be recorded with Prince's new backing band, The Revolution, and '1999' featured the voices of two them, Lisa Coleman and Dez Dickerson, who took it in turns with Prince to sing the couplets. The song reflected the mood of the times, when the cold war had taken a chilly turn and fear of nuclear war was in the air ('Everybody's got a bomb, we could all die any day').

There's also more than a whiff in Prince's lyrics of his background in the pre-millennial, apocalyptic Seventh-Day Adventist Church: the longer album version of '1999' spirals off into a handclapping funk workout, with Prince declaiming, 'Can't run from Revelation'. And there's a curious line in which Prince sings, 'I've got a lion in my pocket, and baby he's ready to roar'. On the face of it, this seems to be a straightforward sexual metaphor, except that in the Bible's Book of Revelation the Lion of Judah is a symbol for the return of Christ. Of course, Prince

being Prince, it's entirely possible that its meaning is both sacred and sexual.

The song's initial release as a single failed to make much impact, however. It was followed up by 'Little Red Corvette', which had enormous crossover appeal, bringing Prince's music to a wider, whiter audience. In 1983, '1999' was re-released and was a hit in several countries. Over the years it has been re-released many times, notably in 1999 itself, when the world was gripped by apocalyptic fears of collapse caused by the Millennium bug and partygoers took solace in Prince's mood of defiant delirium. (Prince had been at war for some time with his record company, Warner Brothers, which owned the master tapes; to prevent Warner from profiting from the song, he re-recorded it in 1998.)

In 1999 Prince (who by now had changed his name to a symbol) recorded a live show, *Rave Un2 the Year 2000*, which was broadcast on American pay-per-view television on the eve of the new millennium, culminating in an extended '1999'. After this, Prince vowed never to play the song again, but he later revived it in live shows; it cropped up during his run of 21 concerts at London's O2 Arena in 2007.

The song has not been widely covered, but a brave few have attempted it. Big Audio Dynamite covered it somewhat feebly in 1992. English electro artist Gary Numan did a sound job of it on his *Machine and Soul* album, released in 1999, exploring – as you'd expect – the song's darker side. Anonymous eyeball-headed West Coast experimentalists The Residents went further, turning the song into a clanging, twisted dystopian vortex on their *Dot.Com* album (2000). American nu-metal band Limp Bizkit murdered it on stage, vocalist Fred Durst basically shouting the chorus while his bandmates thrashed the riff to death. The American singer Beck, who has also covered Prince's 'Raspberry Beret', has incorporated '1999' into his live shows in a version that stays true to its funky roots. There's also a jazz version by Bob Belden and Peter Bernstein on the *Blue Note Plays Prince* tribute album; their big, brassy arrangement is let down by Bernstein's polite-sounding guitar. Meanwhile Prince plagiarized the vocal melody in his own 1986 song for The Bangles, 'Manic Monday': the tune from one song could easily be sung to the riff of the other.

Finally, '1999' returned to the charts in 2016 following Prince's death at the age of 57. No doubt it will continue to get heavy rotation at New Year's Eve parties across the globe in tribute to the man who sang, 'We could all die any day/But before I'll let that happen/I'll dance my life away.'

David Cheal

SMELLS LIKE TEEN SPIRIT

In a small town in Washington state in 1990, you had to make your own amusement. So it was that Kathleen Hanna and her friend Kurt spent an afternoon spraying graffiti on to a Christian teenage pregnancy advice centre and then returned to his rented apartment to drink. One thing led to another: Hanna 'smashed up a bunch of shit' and defaced the walls in marker pen. One of her phrases stuck in his mind. 'Kurt', the scrawl read, 'Smells Like Teen Spirit'. Teen Spirit was, in fact, the deodorant worn by his then girlfriend Tobi Vail, who was Hanna's bandmate in embryonic riot grrrl band Bikini Kill. But, thought Cobain, it could be a song lyric.

Grunge, a form of alienated music on the border of metal and punk, had been around for a while before Cobain and two friends formed Nirvana. But 'Smells Like Teen Spirit', released on the band's second album *Nevermind* in 1991, made it an international sensation. Kurt Cobain's influences included the Pixies and, less fashionably, soft-rockers Boston; the song's elliptical lyrics ('Load up on guns/Bring your friends . . . A mulatto/An albino/A mosquito/My libido') hinted at troubled racial politics and AIDS panic without ever making anything explicit. When he chorused 'I feel stupid and contagious/Here we are now, entertain us' he summed up the new *fin de siècle*. Quiet passages alternated with rage: guitars crunched, drums crashed, Cobain howled. No doubt about it, 'Smells Like Teen Spirit' was the quintessential grunge anthem.

Except, was it? A succession of musicians produced cover versions that, collectively, make the case for the song not being rooted in grunge at all. First up was Tori Amos, an American singer despatched to the UK by her record company in the hope that Britons would appreciate her Gothic confessionals more than her fellow countrymen did. In 1992, Amos was in her pomp: her version replaces Nirvana's *Sturm und Drang* with moody Romantic piano. When Cobain first heard the record, he 'couldn't stop laughing', but he later told MTV it was 'flattering' and claimed that he and Courtney Love danced to it over their morning cereal.

So 'Teen Spirit' could land in a wide musical territory. But no one could have anticipated a metamorphosis a decade after Cobain's suicide in 1994. In 2005 the Canadian-born crooner Paul Anka, best-known for writing the English lyrics to 'My Way', recorded the album *Rock Swings*, recreating the rock canon as swing jazz. Along with 'Eye of the Tiger', 'Jump' and 'Everybody Hurts' is, of course, 'Teen Spirit'. Performing the song at the North Sea Jazz Festival a couple of years later, Anka prowled the stage, clicking his fingers. Where Cobain's 'Hello, hello' had been a wary warning, and Amos's a come-hither, Anka might have been welcoming the Rat Pack into a Las Vegas casino.

It didn't even need words. The Bad Plus, an avant-garde jazz trio matching Nirvana's line-up but with piano for voice, deconstructed the song on a 2003 album. Ethan Iverson, the pianist, starts with the ringing guitar phrase but immediately drops it and warps the melody, taking off into sheets of atonal noise. The clamour drops out to expose Reid Anderson's double bass

nagging away at 'With the lights out/It's less dangerous'; finally the piano returns to the tune.

The song is so well known now that there can be rap versions, comedy versions and a reading from Patti Smith; grunge, as a genre, is ancient history, but 'Teen Spirit' has outlived it. Hanna's graffito never actually became a lyric, but it made a great title.

David Honigmann

18

LA VIE
EN ROSE

Written in a pavement café on the Champs Elysées in 1945, 'La Vie en Rose' was a song whose giddy romance swept the French national spirit from the ashes of the Second World War and sent it soaring around the world. The sole author of this phoenix song was France's 'little sparrow': Edith Piaf.

Born Edith Gassion in 1915 and discovered singing on the streets of Paris's red light district in 1935, Piaf was a singer whose career had taken flight during the Second World War. Though not a conventional beauty, the 4ft 10in diva was a volcano of drama, whose murky tales of murder, abandonment and prostitution were given an added frisson by her guttural vibrato. Although it's often assumed that most of her songs were written for her by men, she wrote more than 100 of them herself and (unusually for the time) wrote many with other women.

Piaf sang through the war as through the tragedies in her personal life, which included the death of her two-year-old daughter from meningitis in 1935 and that of her great love, the boxer Marcel Cerdan, who was killed in a plane crash in 1949. Performing for the occupying Germans as well as her fellow countrymen, Piaf was briefly branded a collaborator. But rumours of Nazi-pleasing were firmly quashed in 1945 when resistance leaders revealed that Piaf had smuggled maps and compasses to French POWs during her prison camp tours. She also posed for photographs with inmates; the photographs were used to create fake identity documents and enabled many prisoners to escape.

After the war, as France sucked up Marshall Plan money and morale-boosting jazz records from the US, Piaf went for a drink with her friend Marianne Michel. The younger singer complained that nobody was writing her any new songs, so Piaf grabbed a piece of paper and dashed off 'La Vie en Rose' for her. The song's central metaphor – of seeing the world afresh, through rose-tinted glasses – was something Piaf knew all about, having been blind for several years in her childhood and claiming to have been cured, aged seven, after the prostitutes working in her grandmother's brothel pooled their earnings to send her on a Catholic pilgrimage.

Michel recorded the song first – a sweet, xylophone-frosted version – with Piaf laying down her own, definitive version two years later. As a hymn to a love affair so beautiful that it allows the singer to forget all *'les ennuis, les chagrins'* (weariness and grief), it saw the tragedienne, like her nation, transcend pain. Piaf's melody whisks you up in its arms and takes you for a slow, dreamy twirl, briefly breaking hold for a few spoken sections before resuming the dance. Her version sold more than 1 million copies and made her name across the Atlantic, where Americans were startled to behold such a tiny woman in a simple black frock, exuding none of the Hollywood glamour to which they were accustomed.

In 1950, Louis Armstrong gave the song a sumptuous treatment with a sleepy trumpet solo that starts out on a bed of solo piano glissandos and blooms against a big-band finale. Singing with one nipple slipping from her metallic négligée in the video, Jamaican supermodel Grace Jones sexed up the tune (with an insouciant guitar strum) for the disco generation in 1977. Fellow disco diva Donna Summer recorded a rather bland version in 1993. Punk growler Iggy Pop added a big slouchy beat to the Armstrong arrangement for the moody version that appeared on his 2012 album, *Après*.

But it was Pascal of Bollywood who gave the best modern account of the song in 2003. Pascal, a French actor and singer (born Pascal Heni) known for reinterpreting Indian cinema songs, duetted with Bollywood star Shreya Ghoshal against a glorious, sari-pirouetting mix of Parisian pavement accordion, sitar, tabla and bansari (Indian bamboo flute). Pascal's version conjures a luminous vision of a blissfully multicultural new France. A small beacon of hope for our dark times.

Helen Brown

19

SOME VELVET
MORNING

There's a glissando of strings, like waves breaking on a shore, then a man's voice, rich and dark, intones the most enigmatic opening lines in pop history: 'Some velvet morning when I'm straight/I'm gonna open up your gate/And maybe tell you 'bout Phaedra/And how she gave me life/And how she made it end/ Some velvet morning when I'm straight.' In response, a woman's voice, light as a summer's breeze, chants an invocation: 'Flowers growing on a hill, dragonflies and daffodils/Learn from us very much, look at us but do not touch/Phaedra is my name . . .'

The year is 1967, the setting is Hollywood. The bass voice belongs to writer/producer Lee Hazlewood, the soprano to his protégée, Nancy Sinatra. The legend they have just spun in vinyl, part rugged country, part fey folk, cloaked in psychedelia by Billy Strange's haunting orchestration, will echo down the years, the puzzle of its lyrics and otherworldly beauty of its sound offering seemingly endless interpretations.

It first appeared on the album of Nancy Sinatra's TV special *Movin' With Nancy*, was then released as a single and finally placed in its most majestic setting, the 1968 Reprise LP *Nancy & Lee*. It crystallizes a moment between the optimism of the 'summer of love' and the darkness on the desert horizon, manifested in rogue hippy Charles Manson. Not for nothing was it voted the best duet of all time by British music critics in 2003.

Barton Lee Hazlewood was born in Oklahoma in 1929, the son of an itinerant oilman, whose wanderings across the south imbued his son with a taste for the cowboy lifestyle and its music. Having served his country in Korea, Lee began working as a songwriter and producer for rockabillies Sanford Clark and Duane Eddy in 1956, hitting upon the novel idea of recording the latter's twanging guitar inside a grain silo.

In 1965, after bonding with Dean Martin over the song 'Houston' and a mutual love of whiskey, Lee was asked by Frank Sinatra to come to the rescue of his daughter's career. Hazlewood duly delivered the smash 'These Boots Are Made For Walkin'', having issued his ingénue with the instructions: 'You can't sing like Nancy Nice Lady any more. You have to sing for the truckers.' Thus recast, Nancy staked her claim to pop immortality and would record another album with the man she described as 'part Henry Higgins and part Sigmund Freud', *Nancy & Lee Again* in 1971.

Her singing on 'Some Velvet Morning', however, is more the voice of an elemental, heightened by the name Phaedra – in mythology, the treacherous wife of Theseus, whose unrequited love for Hippolytus results in his watery death at the hands of Poseidon. Many of Hazlewood's songs, including Nancy & Lee's 'Summer Wine', involve sprite-like beings casting spells on cowboys that result in the loss of senses and spurs, and he based the logo of his record company LHI (Lee Hazlewood Industries) on a classical Greek profile.

But, like the contrast between his vocals and hers, there is another, more carnal interpretation of what those lyrics might mean. Hazlewood's sudden move to Sweden in 1971, at the height of his popularity, added to his mystery – had Frank Sinatra really put out a hit on Lee because Lee and Nancy had grown too close, or was Hazlewood just avoiding the taxman?

This ambiguity has drawn many subsequent artists to their retellings of the myth. Lydia Lunch and Rowland S Howard made the perfect Gothic coupling on their 1982 single. Bobby Gillespie teamed up with Kate Moss to record a version for Primal Scream's 2002 album *Evil Heat*, recently re-released on Ace Records' Hazlewood covers compilation, *Son-of-a-Gun*. Shoegazers Slowdive and proto-grungers Thin White Rope have also taken cracks at the enigma.

But most poignant is the final version Lee recorded before his death from cancer in 2007. On his 2005 swansong LP *Cake or Death*, he duets it with his grand-daughter . . . Phaedra is her name.

Cathi Unsworth

20

HALLELUJAH

It's perhaps the most famous song written by Leonard Cohen, who died in November 2016 aged 82. And yet 'Hallelujah' almost didn't get released; and when it was, it passed almost unnoticed.

In the early 1980s Cohen was going through a fallow period, having not released an album since 1979's *Recent Songs*. He was spending much of his time with his children in the south of France, but eventually a collection of songs came together. In the studio, Cohen took a new approach, with synthesizer-heavy arrangements, and a voice made deeper by '50,000 cigarettes and several swimming pools of whiskey'. Among the songs on the album was 'Hallelujah', an epic, hymnal composition with biblical allusions (David, Bathsheba and Samson are referenced). Cohen later said the song took him two years to write: 'I remember being on the floor, on the carpet in my underwear, banging my head on the floor and saying, "I can't finish this song."'

When Cohen took the album to his record company, Columbia, the suits were not impressed, judging that the album was not good enough to merit release in the US. So in 1984 Cohen released it through the independent label, Passport. It met with little acclaim. But Cohen included 'Hallelujah' in his live shows as he toured the world in the 1980s.

His draft version of the song had around 80 verses, and many of them cropped up in his shows as he shuffled the pack. A 1994 live album features a version recorded in 1988 that is darker than the original, including lines such as these: 'Yeah I've seen your flag on the marble arch/But listen love, love is not some kind of victory march/No it's a cold and it's a very broken Hallelujah.'

The song was gaining traction, but it was properly popularized by John Cale, when his elegant piano-accompanied version was included in a 1991 Cohen tribute album, *I'm Your Fan*. Shorn of the clunky accoutrements of Cohen's version, the song was allowed to shine.

After that, 'Hallelujah' went viral. First to pick up the baton was Jeff Buckley in 1994, whose exquisitely pure tenor voice, recorded with a churchy echo, seemed ideally suited to the song's religious themes. Since then, 'Hallelujah' has become one of the most covered songs ever, up there with 'Yesterday' and 'My Way'.

The hundreds of versions have tended to follow one of two templates: either stripped down and simple – Rufus Wainwright, accompanied, like Cale, only by a piano – or big and histrionic, like Cohen's fellow Canadian kd Lang, whose swooping, soaring rendition became a staple of her live shows; she also adopted Buckley's trick of going up an octave in the chorus.

Inevitably, 'Hallelujah' was picked up by the reality-show juggernaut, with Britain's *X Factor* winner Alexandra Burke going hell-for-leather in a version that reached the coveted Christmas Number 1 spot in the UK charts in 2008. Families up and down the country were doubtless split along generational lines as youngsters went mad for Burke's version while their elders and betters sought refuge in the calm beauty of Buckley, Wainwright and Cale. (Cale's version also popped up in the *Shrek* movie, although the soundtrack album featured Wainwright's rendition.)

Other versions of note include a gorgeous Yiddish version, with loosely – and creatively – translated lyrics, by Berlin-based singer-songwriter Daniel Kahn; and the English singer Kathryn Williams, who brings purity and elegance to the song. Bob Dylan, who was among the first to see Cohen's lyric to the song when they met in Paris in 1984, has covered it many times.

Cohen himself revisited the song on the world tour that he embarked on in 2008 after finding a black hole in his pension fund, bringing new depths of passion to an arrangement drenched in backing vocals and Hammond organ. In a recording made at London's O2 Arena he clenches his fist and closes his

eyes as he sings: 'I'll stand before the Lord of Song, with nothing on my tongue but Hallelujah'.

But what is the song about? *Hallelujah* is a Hebrew word, meaning 'praise God'; but with its reference to Bathsheba, there's sex as well as spirituality in the song. There is no 'narrative'; it is, rather, a series of meditations. As Cohen himself said: 'The song explains that many kinds of Hallelujahs do exist. I say: all the perfect and broken Hallelujahs have an equal value. It's a desire to affirm my faith in life, not in some formal religious way but with enthusiasm, with emotion.'

David Cheal

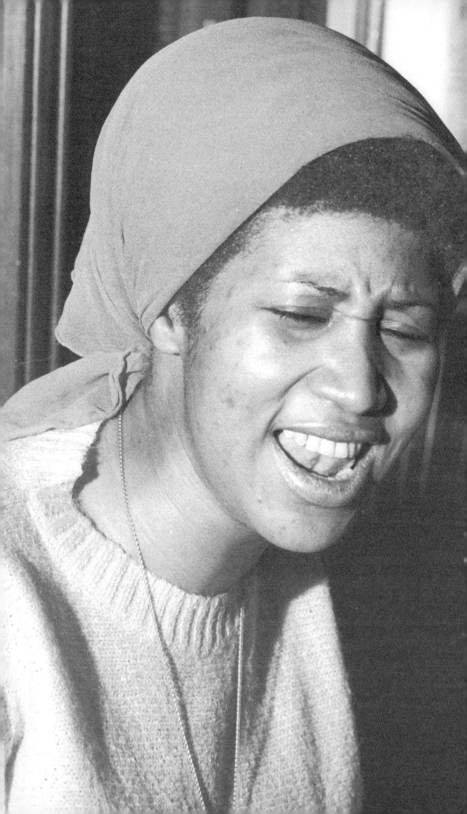

21

AMAZING
GRACE

If you want to summon the soul of black America, invite Aretha Franklin to a solemn occasion and ask her to bring 'Amazing Grace' with her. She performed it at the funeral of soul singer Luther Vandross in 2005, and at the White House in 2014 for President Obama, who sang it himself a year later at the eulogy for Senator Clementa Pinckney, a member of the South Carolina Senate who was killed in a mass shooting at his church.

In 1972, the song marked Franklin's return to gospel music when it gave a title to her live album recorded at the New Temple Missionary Baptist Church in South Central Los Angeles. Bearing witness that day were Rolling Stones' Mick Jagger and Charlie Watts, and gospel legend Clara Ward. Franklin would deliver the song again in seven months, at Ward's memorial service. She even sang it for Pope Francis in 2015.

'Amazing Grace' is touching and beautiful, an apparent hymn of emancipation woven into the fabric of African–American life. But its roots lie in one of the biggest crimes committed against humanity: slavery. This is not a freedom song written by a former slave; it's a redemption hymn composed by a slaver.

'Amazing Grace' began life as a poem. John Newton was born in 1725 in Wapping, east London, going to sea aged 11. In 1744 he was pressed into joining the Royal Navy, and was flogged after trying to desert. He transferred to a slave ship, *Pegasus*,

THE LIFE OF A SONG

but the crew disliked him and Newton was abandoned with a slave trader in West Africa, who handed him to his wife, Princess Peye of the Sherbro people, in what is now Sierra Leone. Peye treated Newton like a slave, too. He later declared himself to have been an 'infidel', 'libertine' and a 'servant of slaves'.

In 1747 he was rescued and sailed to Britain. But the ship was holed in a storm off Donegal and, facing death, Newton prayed to be spared. When he was, he adopted evangelical Christianity, renouncing his profane ways. However, this did not stop him captaining several slave ships until ill health forced him on to dry land in 1754; he continued to invest in the trade.

A decade later he was ordained as a priest in Olney, Buckinghamshire. In 1788 he published a pamphlet condemning his former occupation, supporting William Wilberforce's campaign to abolish slavery. Newton had plenty to repent. His 1779 poem 'Faith's Review and Expectation' was an attempt to do exactly that: 'Amazing grace, how sweet the sound, that saved a wretch like me'. The poem was set to music more than 20 times before it settled on the melody of the folk song 'New Britain' in 1835, ten years after Newton's death.

His lyric was not popular in England, but in nineteenth-century America it gained traction, with added verses that were popular in African–American communities. The first recording of the song was by the Original Sacred Harp Choir in 1922. Gospel giant Mahalia Jackson released it in 1947, and sang it at civil rights marches in the 1960s. It was adopted by the folk movement: Pete Seeger performed it. Judy Collins' celebrated 1970 version sprang from her battle with alcohol abuse: she said the song helped her 'pull through'. Her rendition spent more than a year in the UK chart, where it was joined, in 1972, by a cover from the Royal Scots Dragoon Guards.

Others saying 'Grace' include Elvis Presley (in 1971), Willie Nelson (1976), and even alt-rock band The Lemonheads (1987). There are thousands of versions of 'Amazing Grace'; it is a one-size-fits-all spiritual. When she first performed it, Joan Baez did not know it was a hymn, and surely few of those who enjoy it are aware of the appalling sins its lyric was intended to atone for.

Ian McCann

22

THE LONG
BLACK VEIL

The haunting charms of 'The Long Black Veil' have proved irresistible to many of the world's leading musicians for more than 50 years. They include Johnny Cash, Joan Baez, The Band, Nick Cave, Mick Jagger and the Dave Matthews Band, while many others, such as Bruce Springsteen, have included it in their concert repertoire. That such fine songwriters chose to record this American murder ballad speaks of its calibre, as does its longevity.

The appeal of 'The Long Black Veil' lies in its memorable melody and chorus, and lyrics that tell a compelling story from an unusual perspective. It is related from the grave by a man who was hanged for a murder he did not commit. He could have saved himself but chose not to because his alibi carried a terrible price: 'I'd been in the arms of my best friend's wife.' Death, rather than dishonour for his lover and himself, was his choice. The chorus tells how, ten years on, his grieving lover, wearing a long black veil, still visits his grave 'where the night winds wail'.

The lyrics are masterfully economic yet vivid, the tale unfolding like a film in a mere three verses and chorus. The song was composed in the late 1950s, but evokes an America long past. Its lyricist Danny Dill said he wanted to produce 'an instant folk song', somewhat in the style of Burl Ives, who later recorded it. One of Dill's inspirations was a newspaper story about a mysterious woman who, wearing a black veil, repeatedly visited the grave of film star Rudolph Valentino.

Dill's co-writer was, like him, a southern singer-songwriter, Marijohn Wilkin, whose life was itself the stuff of a country song. Her first husband was killed in the Second World War, and two broken marriages and alcoholism followed, only for her eventually to find redemption in religion. This latter phase of Wilkin's life inspired her to compose the hit song 'One Day at a Time' with Kris Kristofferson.

'The Long Black Veil' was first recorded in 1959, by the honky-tonk singer Lefty Frizzell, who applied his rich baritone drawl to a standard, hopalong country tempo. It proved an immediate hit in the country charts.

The song's greatest champion, however, was Johnny Cash, who recorded it on his 1965 *Orange Blossom Special* album and his *At Folsom Prison* live record three years later. He also included it on a list of what he called '100 Essential Country Songs' that he compiled for his teenage daughter Rosanne in 1973, when she was embarking on life as a professional musician. 'This is your education,' he told her. When Rosanne decided to make her 2009 album, called *The List*, for which she selected 12 songs from her father's favoured 100, she included 'The Long Black Veil'.

It is no surprise that the song's darker qualities attracted the Man in Black, and it was also a predictable choice for The Band on their 1968 debut album, *Music from the Big Pink*. Their own compositions often conjured up a mythic American past, and this song slotted perfectly into the genre.

Perhaps the most radical rendition came from Nick Cave and the Bad Seeds in 1986. They gave it a bluesy, eerie feel and

Cave's voice wails and moans like the cold night winds in Dill's lyrics. Nine years later came one of the most atmospheric versions when the Irish folk band The Chieftains made it the title track of a collection of collaborations with rock stars. They asked Mick Jagger to perform the vocal, and the result is a majestic, slower interpretation, with Jagger delivering a fine blend of country and Celtic vocal styles. Dave Matthews gave it a rockier stamp in 1999, and versions have kept coming since. This ballad of a man who decides to pay the ultimate price for his sin of betrayal seems destined to captivate for years to come.

Charles Morris

I HEARD IT THROUGH THE GRAPEVINE

Motown boss Berry Gordy had a quality control department for deciding whether a song should be released. 'If you had only enough money for this record or a sandwich,' he would ask staff, producers and writers at the hit factory, 'which would you buy?' Or he would play a song through a rigged-up car stereo system to test how it might sound going down the highway. It worked, producing hit after hit.

Sometimes, however, the department missed the best. In 1966 singer-songwriter Barrett Strong came up with an idea for a song based on the expression 'through the grapevine' that he kept hearing on the streets of Chicago. The phrase had its roots in the days of the slave trade. The 'grapevine telegraph' had been the system of communication used by slaves during the American Civil War. Prohibited from learning to read, they passed on news by word of mouth.

Strong took his song to Motown producer Norman Whitfield. Together they worked it up into 'I Heard It Through the Grapevine', a dramatic tale of romantic betrayal. Whitfield recorded a version with The Miracles in 1966 but the Motown committee decided they'd rather buy a sandwich. The following year Marvin Gaye recorded it, but it was Gordy himself who vetoed it as a single.

Eventually 'Grapevine' was released by Gladys Knight & The

Pips in 1967 in a new, more up-tempo arrangement. It was a hit, reaching Number 2 in the charts. Meanwhile, Gaye's version was awaiting its moment. He had recorded the song over five sessions with a backing ensemble that included the Detroit Symphony Orchestra, with Whitfield pushing him to sing in a higher key than his normal range. The song made its way on to Gaye's 1968 album *In the Groove*. When the album was released, 'Grapevine' was picked up by E Rodney Jones, a DJ at Chicago's black community radio station WVON. After the song aired for the first time, Jones told Motown marketing man Phil Jones that 'the phones lit up'. No wonder: listeners were gripped by the ominous intro, the bassline, the brass, the jittery piano, the restrained first-person narrative, the controlled anguish of Gaye's voice. Motown, swayed by public opinion, released it as a single, and it became the label's biggest-selling hit to date.

A couple of years later Creedence Clearwater Revival covered the song in an overblown 11-minute version for their album *Cosmo's Factory*. But it was an English-based female punk band, The Slits, who gave the song its most radical reinterpretation. In tune with the spirit of the times, The Slits happily admitted that they could neither write songs nor play their instruments; nevertheless, they supported The Clash on tour and, in 1979, they were signed by Island Records. Reggae star Dennis Brown had been sent in to produce their first studio session but it became apparent that he did not know his way around the mixing desk.

The Slits gave Brown the boot, and found themselves in the studio with a woman called Rema who had come along with Brown's entourage to help out and make the tea. Rema said she had a bit of studio experience and took over at the controls; together the women worked out how they wanted the song to

sound, giving it a strong reggae vibe. They couldn't afford a brass section, so they sang the horn parts. Then, behind 17-year-old German lead singer Ari Up's vocals, they chanted 'Grapevine, grapevine' over and over – using, as Slits guitarist Viv Albertine later said, 'our real voices, not little-girl voices the way so many girls sing'. This DIY production yielded a recording that's wild, patched-together, ferocious, raw – a total contrast to Motown's pop-factory classic.

Hilary Kirby

BY THE TIME I GET TO PHOENIX

24

Frank Sinatra called composer Jimmy Webb's subtle, mournful ballad 'By the Time I Get to Phoenix' the 'greatest torch song ever written'. Yet when Webb, then a young writer for Motown, presented the tune's three narrative verses to his bosses, they were puzzled: 'Where's the chorus?'

There was no chorus, although not for lack of Motown trying to wrestle one on to it. The song follows the narrator on a road trip to Oklahoma, as he marks out the miles imagining what 'she' is doing as he drives far away from her, for good this time.

After kicking around fruitlessly at Motown, Webb's song ended up with the singer/producer Johnny Rivers, who recorded it in 1966 on the album *Changes*, for his own label. Rivers, who still tours today, considered releasing 'Phoenix' as a single but instead suggested it to a fellow producer who was working with a young singer/guitarist: Glen Campbell. Campbell had had a couple of minor solo hits (although one of them, 'Gentle on My Mind', went on to win a Grammy), and had stepped in on tour with the Beach Boys after Brian Wilson's breakdown.

Campbell was part of the legendary Wrecking Crew, top LA session players working on such 1960s-defining hits as 'He's a Rebel' and 'California Dreamin''. He also possessed a faultless five-octave range. Giving the song to Campbell was an inspired

suggestion. Within a month of Campbell recording 'Phoenix' in 1967, the tune reached Number 2 in the country charts and Number 26 in the pop charts. It became one of the most-covered songs of the twentieth century, attracting artists from the Four Tops to Nick Cave and the Bad Seeds.

The song opened a partnership between Webb and Campbell that was to produce, among many, the pop country classics 'Galveston' and 'Wichita Lineman'. (Webb has been touring with a show called The Glen Campbell Years, a tribute to the singer who is now suffering from advanced dementia.)

Meanwhile some listeners cavilled at the timings ascribed to the 'Phoenix' route, even producing maps to show how improbable they were. 'Sometimes as a writer you come to a decision like that and you just flip a coin,' the composer responded in the 2011 book *Chicken Soup for the Soul: Country Music*. 'You could try "By the Time I get to Flagstaff", but does it work as well?'

Campbell's sweet-tenored account of 'Phoenix' came in at a radio-friendly less-than-three minutes. But just two years later, a monumental 19-minute version emerged on an album from soul singer Isaac Hayes, then a house musician and writer at Memphis label Stax. *Hot Buttered Soul* became the first album to hit high in four charts: R&B, jazz, pop and easy listening, restoring Stax's fortunes after the loss of its artist Otis Redding in a plane crash.

Hayes audaciously opens with a then unheard-of ten-minute rap, inventing an intense back-story for the 'Phoenix' couple. His sensual baritone delivers a cautionary tale for the uxorious: a husband working triple time to please a faithless woman who brags about his stupidity.

As his wronged protagonist packs his car, it's 3:30 in the

morning and Hayes is yet to go anywhere near the song's melody. By the time he does, the length of the recording – there are only four tracks on the album – had overturned the formula of hit-singles-plus-filler that governed the industry's treatment of black albums. Hayes's million-selling refashioning of a country pop hit opened a radical space into which Marvin Gaye, Curtis Mayfield and others soon stepped.

Yet Hayes said that his rapped intro only came about when he found himself performing a first attempt at 'Phoenix' in front of a chattering club audience. 'I figured I'd better do something,' he told the writer Gerri Hirshey. 'I knew they were going to think I was crazy to be doing a song by a white pop singer, so I figured I'd explain. And I started talking . . .'

Sue Norris

25

TOXIC

In 2003 Britney Spears was suffering a bit of a career slump. She had yet to reach her excruciating, head-shaving nadir of 2007, but she needed a hit. The English songwriter Cathy Dennis had penned a new tune, 'Toxic', that she had offered to Kylie Minogue (who had conquered the globe with Dennis's 'Can't Get You Out Of My Head' in 2001). Kylie, inexplicably, turned the song down, so it was offered to Britney; this jerkily insistent Bond-meets-Bollywood electro-dance-pop tune became a world-wide hit and an instant dance-floor filler.

'Toxic', in fact, has four songwriting credits, the other three being Christian Karlsson and Pontus Winnberg (of the production team Bloodshy & Avant) and Henrik Jonback: all Swedes, another example of Sweden's success in the pop industry. A snippet of the song, the propulsive strings, comes from a Bollywood song in Hindi, 'Tere Mere Beech Mein'. (Dennis's demo for 'Toxic', on YouTube, shows how elements such as the twangy James Bond-ish guitar were added later.) So, an American singer had a hit with a song written by an Englishwoman and three Swedes, with help from a tune used in an Indian film; the song was recorded in Stockholm and Hollywood, then mixed in Stockholm. This is the way the pop world now works. In the days of Tin Pan Alley and the Brill Building, jobbing song-writers would sit around a piano bashing out hits but many of today's most popular songs are not so much written as constructed, by multinational teams.

But once a song has been constructed, what's to stop someone from deconstructing it? Here's where the story of 'Toxic' becomes interesting. In 2011 the American singer-songwriter Jayme Dee stripped 'Toxic' down to its essentials in a radical rereading; she can be seen on YouTube with an acoustic guitar and a sultry pout, moaning the song in a slowed-down 3/4 arrangement.

This was not the first time a Britney song had been given the acoustic treatment: for his album *1000 Years of Popular Music*, the folk-rock singer Richard Thompson did something similar to 'Oops! . . . I Did it Again' (another Swedish-written Britney hit, by Max Martin and Rami Yacoub). What Dee and Thompson achieved was almost archaeological, digging through the accreted layers of production to discover that, underneath it all, there is an actual song.

A radically deconstructed 'Toxic' has also been heard in the distant future. In 2014, London's Almeida Theatre staged *Mr Burns: A Post-Electric Play*, a production first performed in Washington DC which imagines a post-apocalyptic future world in which roving troupes of players perform episodes of *The Simpsons* and sing pop songs from the old days. In such a purely oral/aural world, the play's author Anne Washburn suggests, without access to electricity, TV or the internet, survivors would depend on (and also trade) snippets of script or music for their physical, emotional and spiritual sustenance.

The show's score cleverly imagines how popular music might survive in such a future: in fragments. One of the songs that weaves its way through *Mr Burns* (and it's an apt one, given the poisoned state of this blasted world) is 'Toxic', its Bollywood strings transmogrified into an eerie 'Ooh-ee-ooh' vocal refrain. It's pleasing that this curious and vaguely disturbing song found a new life, as a remnant of a half-remembered relic of a half-forgotten past, drifting in a brilliantly imagined future.

David Cheal

26

SMOKE ON THE WATER

It's the song forever being butchered in the bedrooms of novice guitarists. Famed for its iconic riff, Deep Purple's 'Smoke on the Water' is among the most instantly recognizable songs in rock, a fact that has led to its outlawing in scores of guitar shops lest it send the staff into a fit of rage.

'Smoke on the Water' was written on a whim, a reaction to an incident that very nearly ended in tragedy, though it would provide Deep Purple with their biggest hit. It was December 1971 and the band had arrived in Montreux, Switzerland, to make an album in the Rolling Stones' mobile studio. The studio was stationed next door to the Casino, an entertainment complex on the edge of Lake Geneva. While they were there a concert by Frank Zappa and The Mothers of Invention was held in the casino's theatre. Midway through the show a fan fired a flare gun into the wooden rafters, which swiftly caught fire. Zappa stopped the music and directed fans to the exits. Within hours, the building had burnt to the ground. Miraculously, no one was killed.

The members of Deep Purple watched the fire from their hotel across the lake and quickly set about writing a song. It was bassist Roger Glover who came up with the name 'Smoke on the Water' – the working title had been 'Durh Durh Durh' on account of guitarist Ritchie Blackmore's riff. Singer Ian Gillan took charge of the lyrics, writing a scene-by-scene account of what had taken place, from 'some stupid' shooting the flare gun into the air to 'Funky Claude', aka Claude Nobs, the Casino's owner (and founder of the Montreux Jazz Festival), 'running in and out pulling kids out of the ground'.

It's thanks to 'Funky Claude' that the song saw the light of day. Initially, the band had no plans to include 'Smoke on the Water' on their as-yet-unrecorded album, not least because Gillan was worried the title made it sound like a drug song. But when Nobs heard it he said: 'You're crazy. It's going to be a huge hit.'

He wasn't wrong. Appearing on their sixth album *Machine Head* in 1972, 'Smoke on the Water' was released as a single a year later and, thanks in part to the infectious simplicity of Blackmore's riff, is now held up as a classic rock anthem. The guitarist would have to defend the riff against sniffy inter-viewers who suggested his use of just four notes made it too basic to be any good. His response was that they should listen to the opening of Beethoven's Fifth Symphony.

Over the years 'Smoke on the Water' has yielded cover versions ranging from the decent to the inexplicable. In the former category was a charity recording to help victims of the 1988 Armenian earthquake that featured an all-male roll-call of top rockers including Bruce Dickinson, Bryan Adams, Tony Iommi, Brian May and Keith Emerson, and dialled up the rock histrionics to seismic effect.

In the latter was Pat Boone's deeply peculiar samba/big band treatment for *In a Metal Mood* (1997), an album of rock covers that seemed to have been made with the sole intention of showing that this white-bread singer had a sense of humour.

Similarly baffling was the finger-clicking swing-jazz version by the now-disgraced Australian entertainer Rolf Harris for his

LP *Rolf Rules OK*, on which he employed his usual jaunty singing style, even while uttering the words, 'Watch it burn'.

It's a measure of the enduring regard for 'Smoke on the Water' among guitar obsessives that it is repeatedly used in attempts to break the world record for the number of guitarists playing at once. In 2014 Ian Gillan joined scores of amateur rockers in playing the song on the beach in Lyme Regis in the UK, though they failed to beat the record achieved at a festival in Wroclaw, Poland, in 2009 when 6346 guitarists performed it together, led by current Deep Purple guitarist Steve Morse.

After their early ambivalence, the members of Deep Purple have evidently developed an affection for their most famous song, safe in the knowledge that, as long as people play guitar, it will never go out of favour.

Fiona Sturges

27

THE HOUSE OF THE RISING SUN

Surging with idealism, 22-year-old archivist Alan Lomax set off on his 1937 tour of Kentucky with high hopes. His aim was to find songs. Not new songs, but the so-called 'floating' songs that resounded all over the US, entertaining crowds at medicine shows, keeping rhythm for the railroad workers. Funded with a grant from the Library of Congress, he aspired to capture the 'democratic, interracial, international character' of American folk tradition. He wanted to codify and classify the inchoate soundtrack of the country's daily rituals.

Some were more wholesome than others. In the mining town of Middlesboro, he came across 16-year-old Georgia Turner. She sang him a minute-and-a-half of a sliding blues song that described the wicked allure of a devilish institution down in Louisiana: 'There is a house in New Orleans they call the Rising Sun/It's been the ruin of many a poor girl and me, O God, for one.'

Lomax included the charismatic performance in his 1941 collection *Our Singing Country*. He learnt of another recording of 'Rising Sun Blues', made in 1933 by the Appalachian duo Clarence Ashley and Gwen Foster. Here was a true floating song, a morality tale, some speculated, imported from England, resembling folk ballads such as 'Matty Groves' and 'The Unfortunate Rake'.

Whatever its provenance, the song enthralled a generation of artists. Woody Guthrie recorded a version in 1941. Josh White tweaked the lyrics in his 1947 effort, and Lead Belly made two stabs at the song in the same decade.

And then, another generation joined in: the peacenik troubadours, Pete Seeger in 1958, and Joan Baez in 1960. Back in New Orleans, the search was on for the 'Rising Sun'. Was it a bar, a brothel, a boarding house? There was no definitive answer, but plenty of plausible theories. It was a house of ill repute run by a Madame Marianne LeSoleil Levant (get it?) in St Louis Street; no, it was a hotel for 'discerning gentlemen', as a local newspaper ad described it, in Conti Street. The thicker the mystery became, the greater the song's appeal.

Bob Dylan included it on his first, eponymous, album in 1962. His arrangement was copied from Dave Van Ronk, the singer-songwriter claimed. But the song was free-floating now, impervious to ownership claims. In the same year, Nina Simone recorded her first version, a perfect confluence of her own intensity and the song's portentous moralism.

Then the British, like true rebuffed colonialists, got in on the act. The Animals' 1964 version of 'The House of the Rising Sun' was a sensation. Singer Eric Burdon had heard the song in a Newcastle club, and the group responded with an electric (and electrifying) arrangement. Its arpeggio guitar introduction and Alan Price's frantic organ solo remain forever associated with the song. It was released as a single, despite a then-inordinate length of four minutes 29 seconds. Producer Mickie Most conquered his own initial misgivings. 'We're in a microgroove world now,' he explained to all those remonstrating dust bowl hobos. The floating song had travelled a long way.

Watch its mutation on the original Animals video: the group

wear absurd 'Beatles' suits as they circle their way around the drum kit in single file. They look like the kind of nice boys who would not have made it past the entrance of the Rising Sun. Laugh as you like: this, more than the triumphant opening salvo of the early Beatles' singles, really did mark the British invasion of American popular culture. Lomax had been right. The tradition of American folk music deserved a higher place in the pantheon of art, and would one day help conquer the world.

Peter Aspden

28

SHIPBUILDING

A rattle of dry sticks on drums, then piano and double-bass descending in parallel. 'Is it worth it?' sings Robert Wyatt's distinctive, thin voice. 'A new winter coat and shoes for the wife/And a bicycle on the boy's birthday . . .'

In 1982, in a town of mass unemployment, everyone is talking about whether the shipyards might reopen. There is an unspoken subtext: the only reason the yards might again employ men is because Britain is at war with Argentina over the Falkland Islands.

Elvis Costello, who wrote the words of the song while the war was still being fought, is not always subtle in his politics. (When he imagined the then still-far-off death of Margaret Thatcher, in 'Tramp the Dirt Down', the surrounding lyrics were less nuanced than that title makes it sound.) But here he has the lightest of touches. 'Dad,' says a teenager, 'they're going to take me to task [that is, to the naval task force dispatched to recapture the islands]/But I'll be back by Christmas' – an ironic echo of First World War optimism, although in fact by Christmas 1982 the task force was indeed back in Britain.

'Shipbuilding' was pretty much the last time a popular song about war made a mark on the public consciousness in Britain. Vietnam had spawned a whole sub-genre; there were plenty of songs about the Troubles in Northern Ireland. By the time the war on terror rolled round, popular music in the English-speaking world had abandoned political commentary. Iraq and Afghanistan and the surrounding paranoia were nowhere directly addressed.

Although 'Shipbuilding' is specific in its time and setting, it has been covered surprisingly often. Costello's own version has Chet Baker on trumpet, lending the smoky atmosphere of a working men's club. Tasmin Archer released an EP of brightly-sung Costello covers in 1994, leading off with a reading of 'Shipbuilding' that smooths out its unease. Britpop Bowie-obsessives Suede recorded the song in 1995 for a charity compilation. Their reading is faithful, Brett Anderson's glam accent a fair approximation of Wyatt's reedy treble, a guitar solo by Richard Oakes taking the place of Baker's trumpet.

Other memorable versions are rooted in concept albums. June Tabor, from landlocked Warwickshire, has always been obsessed with the sea, and her nautical album *Ashore* includes the song, with Huw Warren's piano navigating around the original melody. And The Unthanks' side-project *Songs from the Shipyards* offers a version in the accents of Tyneside. Adrian McNally sings the verses, while Rachel and Becky Unthank – as the 'women and children' – chorus 'it's just a rumour, just a rumour that was spread around town . . .'. It makes the community's divisions starker than ever.

One reason, perhaps, why Costello's lyrics are so measured is that the political left in Britain was unsure how to react to the war. The initial impulse was to see it as an imperial adventure; on the other hand, there was a risk of being seen as objectively pro the Argentine junta. Hence, perhaps, the decision to focus on the human cost of the conflict rather than explicitly taking sides.

Indeed, although Costello's 2013 song 'Cinco Minutos con Vos', conceived as an Argentine answer to 'Shipbuilding', begins with a dig at Thatcher urging Britons to 'rejoice', its central image is not of conscripts going down with the torpedoed Argentine warship *General Belgrano*. It is of a dissident being thrown out of a plane into the River Plate. 'And down I went down, like the twist of a screw/Down into the silver, above me the blue.' So, was it worth it? The question still unsettles. And the jobs in the shipyards never did come back.

David Honigmann

ROCKET 88

The life of this song is the story of an entire musical genre. 'Rocket 88' was a hit in 1951 for Jackie Brenston and His Delta Cats. Brenston was a saxophonist, the Delta Cats an R&B band led by Ike Turner; together they created an explosive song that is considered by many historians of popular music to be the first rock 'n' roll record.

Among the factors that have led to the singling out of 'Rocket 88' is the fuzzy guitar sound, achieved thanks to a damaged loudspeaker (pop history is littered with damaged speakers: see The Kinks' 'You Really Got Me').

But was 'Rocket 88' actually the first rock 'n' roll record? It's tempting to reduce musical history to a series of key 'moments' but in truth it is a process, and 'Rocket 88' was only the latest in a series of recordings that took the structure of the 12-bar blues and, both figuratively and literally, electrified it. The song's immediate antecedents were the 'jump blues' or 'jump 'n' jive' songs of players such as Chris Powell and Louis Jordan. Check out 'Rock the Joint' by Chris Powell and the Five Blue Flames from 1949, or Jordan's 'Caldonia' from 1945 (and don't get distracted by the subplot involving Jordan being attacked by his wife with a knife). The roots of rock 'n' roll are clearly audible: the bassline, the beat, the energy.

The bassline in all these songs, played on an upright bass,

is a direct descendant of the left-hand in boogie-woogie piano, the blues-based form that became a craze in the 1930s and 1940s, popularized by players such as Albert Ammons, Pete Johnson and Meade Lux Lewis. This music emerged from the logging camps of Texas and Louisiana and has been dated back as far as the 1870s; these camps would have had a shed, a supply of drink and a piano. There were even pianos aboard the trains carrying workers from one camp to the next.

As for the origins of the term 'rock 'n' roll': according to the state of Ohio, which erected a plaque in commemoration, it was popularized by the DJ Alan Freed, who, from 1951, played the music on his *Moondog House Rock 'n' Roll Party* radio show. But the term has history going back long before Freed's days. In 1933 the Boswell Sisters performed, on film, a song called 'Rock and Roll'; in a stylized maritime setting, the three singers sit aboard a mocked-up boat that is rocking and rolling – though this is just one big visual euphemism: the term's origins are sexual. In 1922, for instance, blues singer Trixie Smith sang, simmeringly, 'My Man Rocks Me (With One Steady Roll)'. But 'rock 'n' roll' had connotations that were sacred, too. In a 1910 recording, the black vocal harmony group the Male Quartette sing about 'Rocking and rolling in your arms/In the arms of Moses'.

Even if 'Rocket 88' wasn't the first rock 'n' roll record, it marks a turning point: it's about a car, the covetable Oldsmobile Rocket 88. Boogie-woogie is the sound of a train running along the tracks, a connection made explicit in Louis Jordan's 1946 hit 'Choo Choo Ch'Boogie' ('Take me right back to the track, Jack') but, by the 1950s, black Americans were moving north, earning better money and buying cars. 'Rocket 88' is a song about mobility, with the car also serving as a metaphor for sexual prowess.

As for cover versions: Bill Haley and the Saddlemen (earth-bound predecessors of his Comets) recorded it later in 1951, but theirs is a thin, countryish approximation. In 1958 Little Richard stole the song's piano intro, virtually note for note, for 'Good Golly Miss Molly'. But few have attempted to record 'Rocket 88' because this thrilling, eruptive song is unimprovable.

David Cheal

30

JOHNNY REMEMBER ME

Early in the 1960s, a morbid craze seized hitsville. The charts were haunted by songs such as Ray Peterson's 'Tell Laura I Love Her' (1960), the Everly Brothers' 'Ebony Eyes' (1961), Twinkle's 'Terry' and the Shangri-Las' 'Leader of the Pack' (both 1964) – all eerie evocations of teenage hot-rodders revving up and riding straight to hell. British movies such as *Beat Girl* and *The Leather Boys* were portraying juveniles playing for kicks in car races and bike burn-ups, too – so our moral guardians had to act.

Attempting to suppress further fetishization of the 'live fast, die young, leave a good-looking corpse' credo, the BBC banned these so-called 'death discs'. But Auntie Beeb could do nothing to stop the creepiest of all these fatal 45s: John Leyton's 'Johnny Remember Me' which, despite the BBC censor, went to Number 1 in July 1961, stayed there for six weeks, then left behind its own trail of tears.

The song was born out of a séance held by two of music's most unworldly characters, producer Joe Meek and songwriter Geoff Goddard. The tale of a lonely cowboy haunted by the ghost of his girl 'Who I loved and lost a year ago', the recording was drenched in echo and the disembodied voice of backing singer Lissa Gray, who sounded as if she really was performing from beyond the grave – she was actually standing in Meek's toilet. Leyton was an actor who played a rock star in the series

Harpers West One, and when he performed the song on the show, its rise was unstoppable.

Both Meek and Goddard were obsessed with the occult. Meek claimed to have received a message from 'the other side' about the impending death of his idol Buddy Holly, who died on 3 February 1959. Meanwhile, Goddard was training to become a medium. Their partnership would create a pre-Beatles hit factory for Meek's unconventional recording methods. Like a walking microcosm of the 1960s, Meek, a working-class outsider, set a collision course for infamy. He rose to the greatest of heights with his 1962 transatlantic smash 'Telstar', performed by the Tornados, which earned him both an Ivor Novello Award and a writ for plagiarism from a French composer that resulted in Meek's royalties being frozen.

It wasn't his only misfortune: amphetamine addiction, obsession with his protégé Heinz Burt and an incident in a public toilet that led to his being blackmailed for his then illegal homosexuality cemented his fate. Goddard left in 1965, accusing his collaborator of stealing material. Burt followed soon after, suing for missing royalties. In 1967 Meek took a shotgun to his landlady, Violet Shenton, and then turned it on himself. Again the date was 3 February.

The multiple untimely deaths of those surrounding him became known as 'the curse of Joe Meek'. Burt and Goddard died within a month of each other in 2000, aged only 57 and 62 respectively. Meek's greatest rival Phil Spector, whom Meek imagined to have bugged his studios to copy his techniques, murdered actress Lana Clarkson at his Los Angeles mansion in 2003. The date was 3 February.

Yet Johnny's ghostly girl continues to call. The song has been covered by many who share Meek's aesthetics, including The

Meteors in 1983, Bronski Beat and Marc Almond in 1985, Dave Vanian's Phantom Chords in 1990 and Spell (Rose McDowall and Boyd Rice) in 1993. Nick Moran retold the Meek–Goddard séance in his 2008 movie *Telstar*, with *The Leather Boys* star Rita Tushingham as the medium. They tried to ban her, they tried to bury her, but no one, it seems, can forget her.

Cathi Unsworth

31

RED RED WINE

When the British reggae band UB40 released an album of reggae covers in 1983, *Labour of Love*, it revitalized their career, delivering four hit singles, the biggest of which was 'Red Red Wine'. The group had been known for their British update of the 1970s Jamaican roots reggae sound, and for their loosely political lyrics. Abandoning the latter for the time being, *Labour of Love* served a dual purpose: the band wanted to acknowledge the origins of their sound, as credibility is everything in reggae, and Jamaica's musical history was packed with little-known songs with commercial potential.

The album's success delighted the writers of the songs and brought some their first substantial payday. However, when it came to 'Red Red Wine', UB40's knowledge of musical history let them down: they had assumed that the song was penned by an unknown Jamaican singer. 'Even when we saw the writing credit which said "N Diamond", we thought it was a Jamaican artist called Negus Diamond,' claimed the group's toaster, Astro. The song's publishing royalties did not reach a struggling ghetto resident. It was not written by a Negus Diamond, but a Neil.

Neil Diamond had recorded 'Red Red Wine' in 1967 for *Just for You*, his second album. Business was slow for the jobbing songwriter back then, and he had time to help out in his

father-in-law's haberdashery shop, where things were also slack
– allowing him to write songs while he worked. One was 'Red
Red Wine', which Diamond envisaged as a maudlin country
ballad about drinking to forget. Once his career took off thanks
to composing several smashes for The Monkees, Diamond
enjoyed a couple of hits in his own right before falling out
with his record label, Bang. Once he'd moved on, Bang added
backing vocals and strings to 'Red Red Wine' and made it a
small hit in the US.

Minor success seemed to be the limit for 'Red Red Wine'. In
1968 British soul singer Jimmy James made an orchestrated
version, which scraped into the UK Top 40. In 1970, Vic Dana,
a protégé of Sammy Davis Jr, took a middle-of-the-road cover
to Number 72 in the US, sounding like an anaemic Roy Orbison.
But it was another small hit that changed the song's direction:
a version by Jamaican singer Tony Tribe in 1969.

'Red Red Wine' was Tony Tribe's first record, and he was
such an unknown that the record label credited it to 'Tony
Tripe'. Recorded in the UK, its jerky ska rhythm was anachro-
nistic even then. But it worked somehow, reinventing the song
as a reggae ditty. British skinheads, obsessed with reggae at the
time, bought it heavily, and the record reached Number 46 in
the UK. But while his record pointed to the song's future, sadly,
its singer did not have one: as his second single was being
released, Tribe was killed in a car crash.

The song languished during the 1970s, though country
balladeer Roy Drusky covered it in the style Diamond had
intended. Then came UB40's 1983 revival, which spent three
weeks at Number 1 in the UK, and five years later, topped the
chart in the US. It has since been regarded as a reggae song,
as Elan's 2001 dance hall cut makes clear. Even Neil Diamond

performed it on stage in a Jamaican style, complete with an approximation of the toast delivered by UB40's rapper Astro. In time for Christmas 2016, UB40 squeezed one last drop from the song when the group began marketing their own brand of red wine.

Ian McCann

32

A CHANGE IS GONNA COME

When Sam Cooke wrote 'A Change Is Gonna Come', it was a risky departure from the singer's sensational line of more than 30 crossover pop hits. Not only did it mine Cooke's gospel roots, it was political too. It was the kind of pairing that could, in the US of 1963, jeopardize Cooke's presence on white radio playlists.

Cooke had always admired Bob Dylan's civil rights song 'Blowin' in the Wind'. He pulled it straight into his own live repertoire, but still, as biographer Daniel Wolff wrote, something troubled him: 'Geez, a white boy writing a song like that?' A 2005 biographer, Peter Guralnick, said that Cooke was 'almost ashamed not to have written something like that himself'.

During his long tours across the US, Cooke wrote the song that would be referenced, decades later, in the 2008 'Yes we can' speech made by the first black president-elect of the US: 'It's been a long time coming,' Barack Obama told ecstatic crowds in Chicago. 'Change has come to America.'

The anthem on which Obama drew – 'It's been a long, a long time coming/But I know a change gon' come, oh yes it will' – was released posthumously, as a B-side, in December 1964. That month, Cooke was shot dead at 33 by the manager of a $3-a-night motel, under circumstances that are still disputed. Cooke

had once asked his friend Bobby Womack what he thought of the song. 'It sounds like death,' said Womack.

Cooke had cut the song first as a track for the album *Ain't That Good News*. But between album and single, the song lost a controversial verse alluding to segregation. Ironically, for what was to become a civil rights anthem, he was forced to drop the rebuke: 'I go to the movie and I go down town/ Somebody keep telling me, don't hang around' – lines written after Cooke was arrested at a Holiday Inn when he and his band were denied entry.

Singer Otis Redding, who told a reporter that he wanted to 'fill the silent void' left by Cooke's killing, quickly picked up the song for his album *Otis Blue*. Redding's account, called simply 'Change Gonna Come', is sparer than Cooke's symphonic original – and sticks (though loosely, and more wordily) to Cooke's single.

Rolling Stone magazine ranked 'A Change Is Gonna Come' at Number 12 in its list of 500 greatest songs ever written. In 1992, the film director Spike Lee used the song in his movie *Malcolm X*, deploying it brilliantly in the moments leading up to the activist's assassination.

Covers have ranged from those by Aretha Franklin and Al Green – both steeped in the church – to Seal and Van Morrison. It is a frequent and often incongruous visitor to TV talent shows, although a 2009 *American Idol* finalist, Adam Lambert, invested the song with substance by performing it in make-up and changing a line to 'my change is gonna come'. Lambert, whose open homosexuality had been stoutly ignored by the show, went on to top the Billboard charts, as well as touring in the Freddie Mercury spot with Queen. Lou Reed performed it in 2011 at a benefit for the Clinton Foundation, changing the opening 'I was born by the river in a little tent' to a more plausible 'in this little apartment'.

Obama returned to the song at his inauguration, when Bettye LaVette and Jon Bon Jovi credibly sang it as a duet. Perhaps unsurprisingly, the song did not make an appearance at 2017's presidential inauguration.

Sue Norris

33

DOWNTOWN

In 1965 the man who coined the phrase 'special relationship' died. Winston Churchill was 90 and had lived long enough to witness pop music realize the ties he argued for between Britain and the US.

It was the second year of the British invasion of the American charts. On 23 January, the day before Churchill's death, Petula Clark claimed the tenth British invasion Number 1 with 'Downtown', almost exactly a year after 'I Want to Hold Your Hand', by The Beatles. Clark was the first British woman to top the charts in the US since Vera Lynn's 'Auf Wiederseh'n, Sweetheart' in 1952.

'Downtown' is a perfect example of Anglo-Americana. It was written by the London-based songwriter and producer Tony Hatch after visiting New York. The lyrics describe a wanderer finding solace in Manhattan's noisy streets. Bright orchestral pop gives the bustle an enchanting swing, until at the end a wild trumpet solo muscles in like a young tough from *West Side Story*.

Among the crack musicians was a young Jimmy Page, later of Led Zeppelin, at the time a session guitarist. Hatch meant to offer the song to an American group, the Drifters. But Clark, a former child star whose career had stalled, pounced when he played her an unfinished version. Thus a song full of

Americanisms was immortalized by a singer from Surrey with impeccable tones, the sort of voice that speaks of jolly good shows, not 'sidewalks'.

The British invasion habituated American listeners to pop songs sung in the accents of the old country. But Clark's Englishness was pronounced. The effect was amplified by the lyrics' transatlantic lingo and the tendency of other invasion acts, such as the Dave Clark Five, to use mid-Atlantic accents.

Hatch feared an American audience wouldn't accept Clark's cut-glass pronunciation. But an American record label executive knew better. Joe Smith of Warner Bros, which released the song in the US, understood that its sparkle lay precisely in its mingling of similarity and difference. Hatch's inexpert grasp of American urban terminology, for instance, meant the song should really be called 'Midtown', the actual location of the neon signs and movie theatres it lauds.

The song re-established Clark as one of the UK's biggest singing stars. Covers followed almost instantly, as with the identikit version on Sandie Shaw's debut album a month later. Frank Sinatra attempted a breezy interpretation in 1966, when he was trying to keep up with the new pop generation, but badly misjudged the song by treating it as a joke. Glenn Gould was more respectful in 1967 when he published a dense musicological essay in praise of Petula Clark. 'Downtown', according to the classical pianist, was an 'affirmative diatonic exhortation in the key of E major', while the singer's voice, in a catchier phrase, 'was fiercely loyal to its one great octave'.

The song has continued to bounce back and forth across the Atlantic, as when Dolly Parton turned it into splashy Nashville pop in 1984. But it has resonance outside the Anglosphere too. When Clark made 'Downtown' she was based in Paris, having reinvented herself as a chanteuse after her British career flagged. She recorded a French version of the song called 'Dans le Temps' in which New York turned into Paris. She also sang a German version ('Geh in die Stadt') and an Italian one ('Ciao Ciao'). 'Downtown' isn't just a peerless example of Churchill's 'special relationship', it also marks pop's evolution into a global lingua franca.

Ludovic Hunter-Tilney

BORN IN
THE USA

34

In September 1984, Ronald Reagan was coasting towards re–
election as president of the US. Addressing a crowd in
Hammonton, New Jersey, he paid tribute to a local hero.
'America's future rests in a thousand dreams inside your hearts;
it rests in the message of hope in songs of a man so many
young Americans admire: New Jersey's own Bruce Springsteen.
And helping you make those dreams come true is what this
job of mine is all about,' – the lyrics uncannily like one of
Donald Trump's own tweets.

Springsteen was not pleased. 'The president,' he noted drily
at his next show, 'was mentioning my name the other day and
I kinda got to wondering what his favourite album musta been.
I don't think he's been listening to this one.' And he launched
into 'Johnny 99', a stark ballad from the incomparably bleak
Nebraska, sung from the viewpoint of a multiple murderer.

Assuming Reagan was not a secret fan of *Nebraska*, he had
probably been pointed towards Springsteen by the columnist
George Will, who had recently praised Springsteen's song 'Born
in the USA' for its 'grand, cheerful affirmation'. In fact, 'Born
in the USA' tells the story of a minor criminal who gets 'in a
little home-town jam' and is shipped off to Vietnam, only to
return with PTSD, unable to find employment. Critics musical
and political gleefully fell on Reagan's 'error', confident that

they had a better grasp of the nature of American patriotism than the Great Communicator (who, two months later, carried 49 of the 50 states).

But if Reagan and Will thought that mood trumped content, they were not necessarily wrong. As originally recorded, Springsteen alone with a guitar, the song's anger is transparent. The chorus is flat, affectless. But when he and the E Street Band came to re-record it for the album that would bear its name, they pumped it up. The melody is pushed to the top of Springsteen's vocal range (in the same way that 'The Star-Spangled Banner' crescendos to impossibly high notes) so that the whole song sounds like its own climax. Roy Bittan's synthesizer fanfare is as bright as cocaine. Max Weinberg's drumbeats explode like artillery shells. The song sounds like a Roman triumph.

Many excellent songs have come out of mixing pop and politics; the dangerous combination is mixing pop and politicians. Donald Trump's playlist of campaign songs had their singers rushing to distance themselves from him, from REM to Adele. He entered the Republican convention in July 2016 to the strains of 'We Are the Champions', over protests from Queen's Brian May.

British politicians have had an equally uneasy relationship with pop, from Harold Wilson courting The Beatles with OBEs, to Tony Blair (a lead singer manqué) wooing and being snubbed by everyone from David Bowie to Noel Gallagher. Another former prime minister's penchant for early 1980s Mancunian indie earned him a rebuke from Johnny Marr: 'David Cameron, stop saying you like The Smiths, no you don't. I forbid you to like it.'

According to the moral foundations theory propounded by the American psychologist Jonathan Haidt, political progressives stress 'care and fairness' while libertarians favour 'liberty and fairness', whereas conservatives also respond to 'loyalty, authority and sanctity'. Examining 'Born in the USA' through this lens is revealing. Springsteen is famously progressive, and all rock musicians are secretly libertarian, so 'fairness' resonates throughout the song. But the chorus also sounds like an appeal to in-group loyalty, and the music is stamped with authority. No wonder conservatives – including Donald Trump, who of course played it at his rallies – also respond to it.

Springsteen is still infuriating politicians: in spring 2016 he cancelled a concert in North Carolina in response to the state's new law on transgender access to bathrooms. He does still perform 'Born in the USA', but nowadays it comes with curled, bent acoustic guitar notes, as if Woody Guthrie were performing it in the 1950s. Harder, now, to miss the message. Even for a politician.

David Honigmann

SONG TO
THE SIREN

To the ancient Greeks, they were hybrid creatures, part bird, part woman, who lured sailors to their deaths with the spell of their music. In 1967, singer and songwriter Tim Buckley and poet and lyricist Larry Beckett paid tribute to those deathly seducers with 'Song to the Siren', a haunting ode to doomed love whose story is the stuff of pop legend.

The story began when Beckett wrote the lyric and took it to Buckley's house. Buckley took a look, had his breakfast and within minutes 'Song to the Siren' had emerged, almost fully formed. The following year Buckley, then a figure of some standing for his adventures in folk-jazz-rock, sang it on the last ever episode of *The Monkees* television show, introduced off-camera by Micky Dolenz's dramatically curt 'This is Tim Buckley'. In the YouTube footage, the segment's psychedelic visual effects cannot distract from the song's simple sweet-sadness, Buckley's 12-string guitar ringing out, pure voice singing 'Long afloat on shipless oceans . . .'

But it would be another two years before Buckley released the song. Beckett's lyric featured the line 'I'm as puzzled as the oyster', which attracted derision; Buckley was stung, and abandoned the song. Eventually Beckett rewrote it as 'I'm as puzzled as the newborn child'.

In the meantime, in 1969, country crooner Pat Boone released an absurd, horn-drenched misreading of the tune that opens with him laughing 'Yo-ho-ho and a bottle of rum'. In 1970, Buckley set the record straight, releasing 'Siren' on his experimental *Starsailor* album, which flopped.

Buckley died in 1975 from a heroin overdose and remained a peripheral, cultish figure. But 'Song to the Siren' continued to exert its siren-like attraction to the music cognoscenti. Ivo Watts-Russell, co-founder of the quintessentially indie label 4AD, counted the song among his favourites. In 1983, he was assembling a group of musicians under the name This Mortal Coil to record a single. As a B-side, he wanted 'Song to the Siren'. This Mortal Coil's musicians included guitarist Robin Guthrie and singer Elizabeth Fraser of Cocteau Twins, and it was they who recorded 'Song to the Siren'. Their reading set the template for those that were to follow – drifty, druggy, drenched in reverb, a perfect setting for lyrics such as 'Did I dream you dreamed about me?' Fraser, a Scot, embellished the melody with melismas that seemed part-Caledonian folk, part-Middle Eastern ululation. The B-side became an A-side, and went on to sell half a million copies.

After which, the sirens lay largely dormant until the turn of the century when major figures began to pick up the song. In 2002, Robert Plant covered it on his *Dreamland* album, garnished with his characteristic 'oh-ohs'. In 2007, George Michael opened his gig at the new Wembley stadium by singing 'Siren' from offstage (he later released it as a single).

The solo career of Red Hot Chili Peppers guitarist John Frusciante is decorated with sublime moments of lo-fi brilliance, and his 2009 version of 'Siren' is one of them, catching the song's druggy wave with droning keyboards and a vocal that sounds as if it was recorded in a neighbouring studio. Sinéad

O'Connor's 2010 version is heavily indebted to This Mortal Coil's mystic-Celticism. Bryan Ferry's version for his *Olympia* album (also 2010) is layered, dense and dark; after a while Ferry disappears from the song, leaving the insistent music to exert its pull.

There's a curious and tragic coda to the story. In the mid-1990s, Fraser struck up a relationship with Buckley's son, Jeff; they recorded together (though not 'Siren'). In 1997, after they'd separated, Jeff Buckley was in Memphis, preparing to record songs for the follow-up to his debut album, *Grace*. One evening, he went swimming in a channel of the Mississippi, singing Led Zeppelin's 'Whole Lotta Love' as he swam. His body was found six days later.

David Cheal

36

OVER THE
RAINBOW

A cry of despair from the forgotten, rural heartland of the US, beaten down by years of economic depression. A deep yearning for a technicolour fantasy land where 'troubles melt like lemon drops'. The journey towards a strange old man in a tower who pretends to be more than he is . . .

The year was 1938, and MGM was making a movie of L Frank Baum's 1900 book *The Wonderful Wizard of Oz*. America needed cheering up as it struggled to haul itself from the Great Depression. War loomed in Europe. Two Jewish American songwriters – both sons of immigrants – were commissioned by the studio to knock out a number for 16-year-old Judy Garland. Harold Arlen and Edgar 'Yip' Harburg had already collaborated on hits such as 'It's Only a Paper Moon' and 'Lydia the Tattooed Lady'. Harburg was best known for the song 'Brother Can You Spare a Dime?', which brilliantly captured the human cost of the Depression.

'I grew up in the slums,' Harburg once said. 'I know what it is to have your father come home from the sweatshop after working 12 hours a day.' So he didn't want to write 'a maudlin lyric of a guy begging. I made it into a commentary. It was about the fellow who works, the fellow who builds, who makes railroads and houses – and he's left empty-handed. This is a man proud of what he has done but bewildered that his country with its dream could do this to him.'

Harburg saw the story of *The Wizard of Oz* as a parable about what might be achieved under President Franklin D Roosevelt, if his countrymen rediscovered their hearts, brains and courage and worked together to build a brighter future. He had a passionate belief in the power of music to win hearts and minds. 'Words make you think a thought,' he said. 'Music makes you feel a feeling. A song makes you feel a thought.'

Arlen dreamt up the melody of 'Over the Rainbow' – opening with a bold leap straight up an octave from middle C – while parked outside Hollywood's famous Schwab's Pharmacy. Harburg initially thought the tune too schmaltzy. But he took it to his old classmate, Ira Gershwin, who thought it would work if they picked up the tempo. The sweetness was offset by darker underlying chords.

Garland delivers the song five minutes into the film, yearning to escape the monochrome of Kansas into the vibrant colours of Oz. Producer Louis B Mayer initially wanted to cut it because it slowed the action and his star sang it 'in a barnyard'.

There were also concerns that they wouldn't shift sheet music because that opening octave hop would put the song beyond the range of the average Joe. He was talked around. The song won an Oscar, ultimately voted the best ever song in a movie and the greatest song of the century by the Recording Industry Association of America in 2001. It became Garland's signature song, its optimism increasingly painful as her life imploded and her voice cracked. She gave a hollow laugh as she sang it at her final concert in Copenhagen in 1969, three months before her fatal overdose aged just 47.

Often described as 'America's Song', if not its anthem, 'Over

the Rainbow' has been covered by every jazz singer going since 1939 – in 2016 Gene Wilder died listening to Ella Fitzgerald's version – as well as pop, rock, classical, folk and dance acts. David Bowie reworked it as the chorus of 1972's 'Starman', yearning to escape the sexual restrictions of Kansas-grey England. Jazz pianists Keith Jarrett and Dave Brubeck have both recorded classy versions.

More recently, Hawaiian singer Israel Kamakawiwo'ole had a hit with his 1993 ukulele version, medleyed with 'What a Wonderful World', and capturing the song's naivety and melancholy with a lightness of touch that breezed from a morbidly obese frame. Complications from Kamakawiwo'ole's weight would leave him dead, four years later, at just 38, but his version continued to chart across the world – in 2010 it reached Number 1 in Germany.

In the 1980s the elderly Harburg conceded: 'My generation unfortunately never succeeded in creating that rainbow world, so we can't hand it down to you. But we could hand down our songs which still hang on to hope and laughter, in times of confusion like these.'

Helen Brown

37

ENTER SANDMAN

The riff, a great swaggering beast of a thing, came to Metallica's guitarist Kirk Hammett while he was jamming in a hotel room in the early hours. It was 3am, the spookiest time of the night, when suicides peak and the spirit world is at its most restless. 'Devil's hour' occultists call it: for 3am is the opposite of 3pm, supposed time of Christ's death.

Hammett's inspired, or possessed, moment of insomnia was the foundation for one of the most famous songs in heavy metal. It is 'Enter Sandman', the lead single of Metallica's self-titled 1991 album. Also known as *The Black Album*, this was the LP that marked the California band's ascension to superstar status, selling 16 million copies in the US alone and spending more than 300 weeks in the charts.

'Enter Sandman' is about a boy suffering nightmares after being visited by a macabre Sandman, bringer of dreams in European folklore. The song opens with an ominous acoustic guitar melody, a dark lullaby summoning sleep. Then Lars Ulrich's drums and Hammett's chugging riff rise up like roiling monsters from the deep. Singer James Hetfield's roar comes next, building to a chorus as bleak as any Samuel Beckett stage direction: 'Exit light/Enter night'.

Despite its witching-hour theme, 'Enter Sandman' marked a move towards a crisper, more streamlined sound for the thrash metal pioneers. It was produced by seasoned producer Bob Rock, starting a long and, to diehard fans, controversial partnership with the band. He persuaded Hetfield to simplify his lyrics and made Ulrich improve his drumming. Taken with Hammett's riff, the result is a juggernaut of a song, like the huge runaway truck that tries to mow down the sleeping boy in the song's video.

'Enter Sandman' has entered American popular culture as surely as any American Songbook standard. It has been covered repeatedly – by acts from Motörhead to Björn Again – is regularly played at sports events and was even blasted out as intro music to a 2013 speech by Republican presidential hopeful Rand Paul. It might seem odd that a song about night terrors should be clasped so close to the American bosom – until you realize that 'Enter Sandman' is actually not at all scary. I defy even the most timid reader to flee for the hills as Hetfield growls about 'Heavy thoughts tonight/And they aren't about Snow White'. Hammett's guitar solo at the bridge is pure metal peacockery, not a desperate wail of anguish. The song is a display of power, not an exercise in tension.

Truly chilling music is different. It is higher pitched, highly strung, full of anxiety. Think of the slashing chords of Bernard Herrmann's score for *Psycho* or the shrieking strings in Krzysztof Penderecki's masterpiece of dread, 'Threnody to the Victims of Hiroshima'. The violin is the prime generator of fear here. Celebrated as the musical instrument closest to the human voice, its screeching tones evoke the scariest sound of all, the scream.

The gap between the ostensible scariness of 'Enter Sandman' and its actual non-scariness has been ably exploited by parody songs, such as a twinkle-toed big-band version by veteran smoothie Pat Boone. But there is a sinister twist to the tale.

After the invasion of Iraq in 2003, 'Enter Sandman' was

among a perverse playlist of songs used by the American military to torture prisoners, blasted at excruciating volume with strobe lighting for 24 hours at a time. It was the US's very own 3am moment, the dark side of the 'war on terror'. Hetfield's indifferent response to the nightmarish misuse of his song is far scarier than his cartoonish lyrics. 'It's just a thing,' Metallica's singer said. 'It's not good or bad.'

Ludovic Hunter-Tilney

WADE IN
THE WATER

When *Melody Maker* interviewed the British blues-rock musician Graham Bond about his album *The Sound of 65*, the sax and organ player didn't bother toning down his usual brash certainty. Explaining why he had opened and closed the tune 'Wade in the Water' by ghosting a Bach cantata on Hammond organ, the Graham Bond Organization showman was blunt: 'We're playing the blues of today and I can get away with playing practically anything.'

The same scarcely applied to those unnamed men and women who might have sung the original spiritual out of which Bond's raucous account grew. In mid-nineteenth-century America, the song's biblical references to the Israelites' flight out of Egypt – 'Who's that young girl dressed in white/Wade in the water/Must be the children of the Israelite/God's gonna trouble the water' – were reputedly pulled into service as code to help slaves planning to escape. Harriet Tubman, a former slave and leading 'conductor' on the so-called underground railroad that helped slaves escape in the 1850s, is said to have sung the spiritual at innocent-seeming gatherings – the lyrics intended to remind would-be fugitives to take to the water to throw pursuing bloodhounds off the scent.

In 1866 the Fisk Free Colored School opened in Tennessee, named after the abolitionist General Clinton B. Fisk. The school, now a historically black university, swiftly fell into debt. To

139

raise money in the 1870s, it mounted a successful tour by the Fisk Jubilee Singers, students who performed traditional spirituals, including 'Wade in the Water', to white and black audiences alike. The singers also helped bring credence to spirituals as a concert form.

In 1901 the song was published for the first time, in a collection of the Fisk Jubilee Singers' work. The preface hoped the book would be useful, especially as 'it has been found almost impossible for the Caucasian to successfully catch and reproduce the peculiarly characteristic rhythm and harmony of melodies of this type'.

We'll never know the exact cadences and rhythmic inflections of the slave-sung originals. A clue might come from the scratchy field recordings folk song collector John Lomax made of 'Wade in the Water' for the Library of Congress in 1939 and 1940. They cemented the song in the folk repertory, but by then the Fisk Jubilee Singers and their songbooks had spawned the rich harmonies, call-and-response patterns and swooping bass of commercial gospel.

The first recorded version of 'Wade in the Water', by the Sunset Four Jubilee Singers in 1925, was typical of the genre. The Charioteers' 1939 recording was even glossier, and by the time the Golden Gate Quartet recorded the song in 1948 individual voices were prominent, prefiguring the doo-wop groups of the rock and roll era. 'Wade in the Water' entered the soul-jazz repertory in the late 1950s. When musicians took to quoting the first bars of the melody while soloing on other tunes, they were alluding to the song's coded past life, using it as a signifier to the hip and racially conscious.

The first modern jazz recording was a swaggering arrangement by Johnny Griffin's Big Soul Band in 1960. By 1965,

Graham Bond had hold of the song: the album version was short, but live it could take ten minutes before Jack Bruce on bass and drummer Ginger Baker slammed in with gritty R&B and a template for heavy rock trio Cream.

A year later the opening brass fanfare, driving tambourine, soul-stirring handclap and joyful piano of the Ramsey Lewis Trio's million-selling version became a longstanding club classic and a northern soul staple.

Secular vocal versions of 'Wade in the Water' include Marlena Shaw's jaunty 1966 cover – another northern soul favourite – under the title 'Let's Wade in the Water'. Veering straight off message, Shaw declares, 'You know you got me sailing from midnight to dawn'. And the original lyrics were bound to appeal to original 'Hound Dog' singer Big Mama Thornton, who never could pass by a double entendre. She recorded it in 1968: 'See that girl dressed in white, she like to wade all night'.

Lewis, who played London's Ronnie Scott's club in February 2016, still performs 'Wade in the Water' when he tours. And in March 2016, PJ Harvey drew on the original lyrics of 'Wade in the Water' to build the chorus of her anti-pollution song 'River Anacostia', thus keeping the song's roots in protest alive.

Mike Hobart

DARK WAS THE NIGHT, COLD WAS THE GROUND

This song is currently hurtling through space at about 37,000mph, having travelled more than 13 billion miles in 38 years. After flying past Jupiter and Saturn, in 2012 it became the first man-made object to reach interstellar space (although according to some scientists it is still in the solar system, as it has yet to pass through the Öpik-Oort Cloud, which will take another 14,000 to 28,000 years).

When the Voyager 1 probe was launched on 5 September 1977, a gold-plated 12-inch phonograph disc was attached to it, encoded with messages from humanity, greetings in 55 languages, animal calls, tribal songs and music, as well as encrypted photographs, for the benefit of any civilizations that might eventually encounter the craft. Helpfully, a stylus and diagrammatic instructions were included to assist with playback.

Among those on the committee who chose the music for the disc was the cosmologist, astrophysicist and popularizer of all things astronomical Carl Sagan (whose landmark 1980 TV series *Cosmos* was remade in 2014). The choices he and his colleagues made included the usual suspects – Bach, Beethoven, Mozart. But there's also an odd little tune on the disc, recorded in 1927 by a Texan preacher and street-corner blues singer, Blind Willie Johnson. 'Dark Was the Night, Cold Was the Ground', adapted from an eighteenth-century hymn, is wordless, consisting only of Johnson's slide guitar and his resonant, gospelly, moaning hum. The song was picked by Sagan, who said it concerns a situation Johnson – and humanity – faced many times: 'Nightfall with no place to sleep'.

Johnson, who made 30 commercial recordings, died in poverty after his house burnt down in 1945, and received little recognition for his music in his lifetime. In the years that followed, artists such as Eric Clapton and Bob Dylan covered his songs – or, rather, his interpretations of traditional songs. Led Zeppelin recorded a thunderous version of his 'It's Nobody's Fault But Mine', although they failed to credit him. Umpteen singers and bands have recorded his 'John the Revelator'.

But 'Dark Was the Night, Cold Was the Ground' remains his finest few minutes, and although, as Sagan pointed out, it is a very earthbound song, it has an ethereal quality that seems to make it appropriate for the vastness of space. The crackliness of the recording only adds to its sense of remoteness. Jack White, formerly of The White Stripes, has said that it is 'the greatest example of slide guitar ever recorded'. Slide virtuoso Ry Cooder recorded an exquisite instrumental version in 1970; it later formed the basis of his theme tune for the 1984 film *Paris, Texas*.

And now, as it speeds silently through space, the planets have aligned favourably for the song, and for Johnson himself. In 2016 a tribute album (on Alligator Records) was released featuring artists such as Tom Waits, Derek Trucks and Maria McKee performing 11 of Johnson's songs. The album, *God Don't Never Change: The Songs of Blind Willie Johnson*, was an eight-year labour of love for its producer, Jeffrey Gaskill, a long-time Johnson devotee. As well as setting up a Kickstarter campaign to fund the album, Gaskill went back to what remains of a

143

house where Johnson lived in Marlin, Texas, and, with permission, salvaged three wooden boards that had fallen from the structure. These lengths of yellow pine were crafted by a luthier into ten 'cigar-box' (i.e. rectangular) guitars, which were sold to raise more funds.

On the album, 'Dark Was the Night' is sung by Rickie Lee Jones. She reinstates the words to the hymn, written in 1792 by English clergyman Thomas Haweis; it's haunting.

David Cheal

THIS LAND IS YOUR LAND

When he joined members of Vampire Weekend on stage in Iowa in January 2016 to sing 'This Land Is Your Land', Bernie Sanders (mercifully off-mic) was following in a long political tradition. The Vermont senator might be surprised to learn, however, that Woody Guthrie's song – widely regarded as an alternative national anthem for the US – has been co-opted by Republicans as well as Democrats since the bard of the Great Depression first put pen to paper in February 1940. George HW Bush employed it for his 1988 campaign, and its patriotic poetry ('I saw below me that golden valley', etc.) was deemed sufficiently freedom-loving for inclusion in cold-war school songbooks.

Right-wingers, though, gloss over the verses berating 'private property' and bemoaning the queues outside 'the relief office'. On the political left, the song has been cherished, from George McGovern citing it in 1972 to Bruce Springsteen and an 89-year-old Pete Seeger playing it at the 2009 Obama inaugural celebration. (They sang the less revolutionary variant about 'No trespassing'. Sanders just stuck to the poetry.)

Guthrie wrote the lyrics in response to Irving Berlin's nationalistic schmaltz 'God Bless America', as sung in 1938 by Kate Smith, the first lady of radio, while storm clouds brewed in Europe. The initial chorus, 'God blessed America for me', soon morphed into 'This land was made for you and me'. Guthrie set the words to a tune derived from the Carter Family's 'When the World's on Fire' (itself based on the Baptist hymn 'Oh, My Loving Brother') and their similar number, 'Little Darlin' Pal of Mine'. He recorded it in 1944 for Folkways but it was not released until 1951, minus the part knocking private property. Guthrie's acetate with this contentious section was only rediscovered in 1997.

The song has been covered by artists from the Kingston Trio to Johnny Cash. Its oppositional attitude makes it the granddaddy of all protest songs, an inspiration to singers from Bob Dylan to Tracy Chapman. YouTube footage from 1985 has the Boss introducing it as 'the greatest song ever written about America . . . [it] gets right to the heart of the promise of what our country was supposed to be about'.

Yet it took Native American Henry Crow Dog to point out

its colonial overtones. When the Lakota Sioux chief told Pete Seeger in 1968 that 'this land belongs to me', the veteran folkie was so abashed that he commissioned another verse from the indigenous perspective: 'This land was stole by you from me'.

A staple of the Farm Aid benefit concerts, the song has enjoyed plenty of exposure in the twenty-first century. The retro-soul group Sharon Jones & the Dap-Kings did a startlingly brassy rendition for their 2005 album *Naturally*; in 2012, Neil Young and Crazy Horse included a gloriously ragged one on their *Americana* album. Possibly the most successful recent reworking is by My Morning Jacket, their twangy then squally guitars underpinning Jim James's mellifluous vocal on a 2014 commercial for an adventure clothing brand that also raised money for conservation.

Given its canonical status and contested legacy – as Robert Santelli writes in *This Land Is Your Land: Woody Guthrie and the Journey of an American Song*, 'No other American standard at the same time praises and dissents, celebrates and castigates, loves and warns' – parodies were inevitable. The most notorious broadside came in 2004 when the Californian animators JibJab had a satirical dig at both Dubya and John Kerry ('This land will surely vote for me'). From the resulting legal scrum it emerged that the copyright on 'This Land', or at least a version of it, may have lapsed in 1973. In which case, fittingly, this song really is 'for you and me'.

Richard Clayton

BECAUSE
THE NIGHT

Patti Smith, punk-poet queen of the US, isn't known for being a crowd-pleaser. She first made her name in the 1970s on the New York performance poetry circuit, doing readings to a back-drop of squalling feedback courtesy of guitarist Lenny Kaye. Her first album, *Horses* (1975), with its opening line 'Jesus died for someone's sins, but not mine', brimmed with stream-of-consciousness fury and wilfully ignored punk's self-imposed rule about two-minute songs, instead delivering ten-minute epics that referenced her literary heroes, among them Rimbaud, Blake and the Beat poets. Certainly, a hit single was never part of the plan.

Yet there is one track in the Smith catalogue that, at concerts, makes the quietly faithful leap about and punch the air. It tells of hedonistic abandon, red-hot desire and love as 'an angel disguised as lust'. With its big chorus and romantic proclamations, 1978's 'Because the Night' is, to all intents and purposes, a power ballad – more Pat Benatar than Baudelaire.

The song was initially conceived not by Smith but by her fellow New Jerseyite Bruce Springsteen. He began writing it in 1977 in Los Angeles during the sessions for his *Darkness on the Edge of Town* LP. But, after composing the melody and the chorus, he abandoned it.

Down the corridor from Springsteen, Smith and her band

were working on their 1978 LP, *Easter*. Smith's producer, Jimmy Iovine, was simultaneously engineering for Springsteen and could be found darting frantically between the two studios. It was his idea that Springsteen offer the song to Smith.

Legend has it that Smith wrote the verses while waiting for a phone call from her new boyfriend, Fred 'Sonic' Smith, with whom she would later settle down and have two children. Released as a single, the song was a huge hit on both sides of the Atlantic. In her book *Just Kids*, she recalls ambling around downtown Manhattan with her friend and ex-lover Robert Mapplethorpe and hearing 'Because the Night' blaring out of successive storefronts. 'Patti,' he remarked, archly. 'You got famous before me.'

If Mapplethorpe was supportive of Smith's success, some of her fans were less approving and accused her of selling out. Not that she cared: 'I liked hearing myself on the radio,' she told *New York Magazine*. 'To me, those people didn't understand punk rock at all. Punk rock is just another word for freedom.'

Springsteen has always credited Smith for turning the song into a hit, though he hasn't altogether relinquished his stake. He frequently performs it at concerts, replacing the sex-induced sweat of Smith's version with a different kind of perspiration – that of the working man labouring under the hot sun. It has become his go-to track for starry duets: in 2004 he sang it with REM's Michael Stipe in a 'Vote for Change' concert in support of the would-be president, John Kerry, and has performed it multiple times with Bono.

Indeed, one of the song's more startling renditions came during a Rock and Roll Hall of Fame 25th anniversary show, when Bono invited both Springsteen and Smith to perform it together with him. On this occasion they went with Smith's lyrics.

The song has proved to be cover-version catnip to other artists. 10,000 Maniacs did an elegant if somewhat vanilla interpretation for an MTV Unplugged performance in 1993, complete with a string section. Garbage restored the heat and the power for their 2013 collaboration with Screaming Females, released to coincide with Record Store Day.

At 70, Smith still delights in playing the song in her live shows, a joyful explosion of lust shoehorned between darker tales of misfits and outsiders.

Fiona Sturges

MY FAVORITE THINGS

For a while in the late 1950s and early 1960s New York jazz musicians competed to turn unlikely tunes into modernist gems: Sonny Rollins, for example, transformed 'I'm an Old Cowhand'. But fellow saxophonist John Coltrane's choice of 'My Favorite Things' as a 13-minute album track seemed perverse. The song's waltz tempo, unusual structure and frothy emotional palette were at odds with prevailing jazz practice.

The song came from the Rodgers and Hammerstein Broadway show *The Sound of Music*, where it was first performed in 1959 by Mary Martin and Patricia Neway. Would-be nun Maria is told by her abbess she is to work as a governess for the von Trapp family. The now so-familiar 'Raindrops on roses and whiskers on kittens/Bright copper kettles and warm woollen mittens' are part of a nostalgic list that Maria summons to cheer herself up. The shifting cadences and final reassuring shift to a major key capture brilliantly the two women's emotions.

McCoy Tyner, Coltrane's then pianist, recalled that a song-plugger showed Coltrane the sheet music. Intrigued, Coltrane put it in his set, reworking it as a minor-key vamp. In October 1960 he made it the title track of his album, improvising on soprano sax on the raga scale introduced to him by sitarist Ravi Shankar. Coltrane's choice of soprano reintegrated the instrument into jazz, where it had long been out of favour. An edit released as a single pushed the album to sell 50,000 copies in its first year – remarkable for a jazz LP. One commentator likened the track to 'a hypnotic eastern Dervish dance' and Coltrane's refashioning helped to filter Indian music to a wider audience, five years before The Beatles' 'Norwegian Wood' became the first Western pop song to use a sitar. The Doors' guitarist Robbie Kruger used elements of Coltrane's vamp to spice up the instrumental breaks of the band's 1967 hit 'Light My Fire'.

In 1965, Hollywood picked up the stage show to release one of the most successful musical films ever, with Julie Andrews as Maria delivering the definitive version of 'My Favorite Things'. The film shifts the song from the stage version's abbey to Maria's new bedroom, where she comforts the von Trapp children during a thunderstorm. It was a perfect vehicle for Andrews' precise, reassuring and slightly prim English cadences, and possibly a greater comfort to the children than 'The Lonely Goatherd', the song assigned this duty in the original stage musical. Many subsequent stage productions have kept to this reordering.

The song has become a Christmas staple, ranging from Jack Jones's version in 1964 to Mary J Blige's cover on her 2013 *Mary Christmas* album. The Danish film director Lars von Trier turned the sentiment on its head in his 2001 film *Dancer in the Dark*, starring the Icelandic singer Björk. Here the song takes place – haltingly, miserably – in a prison cell as Selma, Björk's character, faces death.

Lady Gaga performed the song at the 2015 Oscars as part of a medley marking the 50th anniversary of *The Sound of Music*. Julie Andrews joined her on stage at the close of her tribute, but composer and lyricist Stephen Sondheim called Gaga's performance 'a travesty'. Several parodies of the jaunty original

have done the rounds, including a 'senior' version that rails at 'thin bones and fractures and hair that is thinnin''. Of the many jazz versions, guitarist Grant Green's perfectly weighted 1964 cover stands out.

Coltrane himself repeatedly reworked the piece, burrowing ever deeper into phonics and abstraction. The renditions captured on his album *Live at the Village Vanguard Again*, and his final live recording *The Olatunji Concert*, are intense epics that take the song into new and uncharted territory. Compared with the stage-show original, Coltrane's 'Favorite Things' becomes almost unrecognizable.

Mike Hobart

BALTIMORE

'Hard times in the city, in a hard town by the sea.' Thus Randy Newman sums up the city of Baltimore, Maryland on this song from his 1977 album *Little Criminals*. Newman is renowned for his darkly comic songwriting – also on the album is the irony-drenched 'Short People' – but on 'Baltimore' he plays it straight: this is a threnody for a hardscrabble town in the throes of de-industrialization.

Apart from its grim lyrics – hookers, drunks, hopelessness – what is interesting about the song is that it takes an age to reach the chorus. A piano motif circles, the tension builds, until relief of a sort finally arrives when the drums kick in properly and Newman stretches out with 'Oh, Baltimore'. (His studio band, incidentally, included several members of the Eagles.) Eventually Newman's lyric concludes that the only thing to do is to escape, so he packs a family in a 'big old wagon' and sends them off to the mountains, never to return.

The following year, the song was picked up by Nina Simone and it became the title track of her *Baltimore* album. Although her reggae treatment smoothes out the contrasts between verse and chorus that distinguish Newman's original, it nevertheless conveys a deep sense of unease.

This, however, is as nothing compared with the profound mood of despair that inhabits another reggae version, released

in 1979 by Jamaican band, The Tamlins. Propelled by the im-
maculate rhythms of Sly and Robbie, the Tamlins' treatment
brings an almost biblical quality to the song.

Over subsequent decades 'Baltimore' has been covered in a
kaleidoscope of musical styles that testifies to its flexibility and
durability. It was included in 2001 on a posthumously released
EP by Scottish singer Billy Mackenzie, whose take on it is almost
abstract – a wash of synths, and Mackenzie's vocal delivery
eschewing his customary hysterics in favour of something
dreamy and distant. For years it was also a staple of David
Gray's live repertoire, his version adding urgency through a
pulsing beat.

Today, Newman's portrait of Baltimore seems just as pertinent as it did when he wrote the song in the 1970s. The TV
series *The Wire* reflected a city that has never recovered from
the loss of the old heavy industries (90 per cent of local jobs
are now in the low-paid service sector), while *Serial*, the podcast
about the murder of 18-year-old Baltimore high school student

Hae Min Lee, touched on the city's high crime rate. Baltimore's homicide figures, though now declining, still make grim reading – 217 recorded murders in 2014 gave the city the fifth-highest murder rate in the US for cities with populations over 100,000.

Newman himself has received some criticism from Baltimore's citizens and civic authorities for painting such a bleak picture of their city. In fact the lyrics had sprung from a fleeting visit, and he later told the *Baltimore Sun*: 'I couldn't legitimately defend my extensive knowledge of the town. The song just came out.'

There's also a tragic postscript to the life of this particular song. Beneath Newman's version on YouTube are various comments from viewers, one of which reads: 'King Steelo brought me here. RIP.' This is a reference to the rapper Capital Steez, whose track 'Hard Times' (featuring Dirty Sanchez) is based on a looped sample of Newman's piano riff and vocal. The 'RIP'? In 2012, Capital Steez – real name Courtney Everald Dewar, Jr – killed himself by jumping from a building in New York's Flatiron District. He was 19. Hard times in the city.

David Cheal

THE CHAIN

In early 1975, two Americans, Lindsey Buckingham and his girlfriend Stevie Nicks, had just joined a once-famous British blues band now down on its uppers. Buckingham, a perfectionist, buzzed around showing the other members how to play their parts on the songs he was bringing to the project. The bassist was unimpressed. 'The band you're in is Fleetwood Mac,' John McVie told him. 'I'm the Mac. And I play the bass.' And that – as Mick Fleetwood, who was the Fleetwood, records in his autobiography – was that.

A couple of years later Buckingham and Nicks had been integrated into the band, and the new line-up had a successful album under their belt. It was now Fleetwood and McVie together who laid down the signature bass-and-drums riff that would define what was (with all due deference to former members Peter Green, Jeremy Spencer, Danny Kirwan and Bob Welch) the high-water mark of Fleetwood Mac: 'The Chain', from their globe-conquering album *Rumours*.

Fleetwood Mac were in the throes of romantic geometry so complex it would have bemused the Bloomsbury Group, and recording in a Sausalito studio in a blizzard of liquor and cocaine. All of them were writing bitter songs about each other. Stevie Nicks essayed a song she called 'The Chain'. 'I'm down on my knees/Begging you please/Baby don't leave me', she sang –

presumably to Buckingham. In demo form, at least, the song is pretty but abject.

At the same time, Christine McVie, John's by now former wife, was working on 'Keep Me There', a throwback melodically to her solo album of a few years previously. The opening may have been nugatory, but the chord progression up into the chorus had a driving tension. And three minutes in, her ex–husband let fly with that ten-note bass riff and the song raced through an extended coda, with Christine McVie playing jazzy electric piano.

Nearly all the elements were there. The two songs were forged together. New lyrics emerged, turning the submission into defiance. 'Damn your love, damn your lies', Nicks now sang. The sound-world of the song became bleaker. McVie's keyboards were toned down. To knit the whole thing together, Buckingham recycled the instrumental guitar passage that opens 'Lola (My Love)' from his and Nicks's earlier *Buckingham Nicks* album. The resulting amalgam simultaneously hymned the pain of personal separation and the strength of community within the band: 'I can still hear you saying/You would never break the chain.' It was the only song from this line-up credited to all five members of the band.

Many songs from *Rumours* were released as singles, but not 'The Chain'. In the UK, though, the song achieved ubiquity when the BBC used it as the theme music for its Formula One coverage – the Doppler rush of the instrumental break perfectly mirroring the head-turning swivel of watching race cars. This must have delighted Fleetwood, at least, a car enthusiast from his youth.

Cover versions are surprisingly rare. The Saskatchewan hair metal band Kick Axe fuzzed the riff into unintelligibility.

Florence and the Machine performed it at Glastonbury in 2010, casting around valiantly for the appropriate key but fully channelling its tribal intensity. American country-folk singer Shawn Colvin, tasked with reproducing the song for a 1998 track-by-track version of *Rumours*, made 'The Chain' slinky and soulful; her take fades out just before the bass riff. By contrast, the Los Angeles punk experimentalists Liars, on *Mojo* magazine's *Rumours Revisited*, doubled down on the darkness: their reading is glitchy, murky, obsessive – and again, riffless.

But the world of hip-hop can tell a powerful riff when it hears one. Cleveland rappers Bone Thugs-n-Harmony's 'Wind Blow' is essentially freestyle rap over a more-or-less unchanged middle section of 'The Chain', foregrounding the bass melody. A more ingenious homage came in 'Up Your Speed' by the British rapper Sway DaSafo. His song is a tribute to automotive antisocial behaviour, with a video full of souped-up monster cars performing doughnut handbrake turns. It ends with just a snatch of the outro from 'The Chain', combining the band's imperiousness with a cheeky nod to Formula One. Fleetwood Mac themselves fell out, broke up, recruited new members, grew up, and eventually reunited in their five-piece form. The centrepiece of their live sets is still, inevitably, 'The Chain'.

David Honigmann

45

IKE'S RAP II

The Tennessee-born musician and actor Isaac Hayes was a man of many parts. He started out as a songwriter for the Southern soul label Stax in the 1960s, penning hits for the likes of Sam & Dave. Then his own genre-bending albums, mixing a sensitive 'lover-man' persona with a lush cinematic sound, won Grammy awards in the early 1970s. In the meantime, his acting career took him from being a figurehead of so-called Blaxploitation movies such as *Shaft* to stealing the show in the scurrilous 1990s cartoon *South Park* as the voice of Chef.

Generations of rappers have been inspired by Hayes's forceful character and taste for blingy gold chains. Yet one of his most lingering musical influences is the sonic odyssey that the strings score of his 1971 confessional 'Ike's Rap II' has subsequently gone on – not so much the life of a song, as the life of a sample.

It featured first on Hayes's double album *Black Moses*, a record that includes downtempo, extended ruminations on Bacharach & David numbers such as 'Walk On By'. Those tracks proved instructive when the British band Massive Attack – founders of the racially diverse Bristol scene of the 1990s – were mapping out their 'dance music for the head, rather than the feet'. A moody synthesis of stoner beats and melancholy snippets, muttered raps and gospel-infused singing, the style came to be known as 'trip-hop', and the strings from 'Ike's Rap II' are integral to not one but two of its most memorable songs, Portishead's 'Glory Box' and Tricky's 'Hell Is Round the Corner'.

Portishead was the project of Massive Attack's former tea boy, Geoff Barrow, while Tricky (aka the erratic rapper Adrian Thaws) was a key contributor to Massive Attack's debut album, *Blue Lines*. Their closeness explains why Barrow and Thaws allegedly came to be squabbling at the 1995 Mercury Prize bash over who initially sampled Hayes's aching strings and remorseful rhythmic progression.

'Glory Box' was released in August 1994 on the album *Dummy*. 'Hell Is Round the Corner' followed the next February on *Maxinquaye*. The principals disagree about who made the earlier demo, and when one first played his effort to the other. Gentlemen, please, it really doesn't matter: both tracks are touched by greatness.

Sounding retro and modern, as it runs John Barry-like atmospherics into a crescendo of dubby bass, 'Glory Box' has a timeless poignancy. It could be the *cri de coeur* of every girl James Bond ever stood up, with the singer Beth Gibbons unforgettable as the leading lady.

'Hell Is Round the Corner', meanwhile, is a complex weave of paranoia and pleasure. 'Let me take you down the corridors of my life,' Tricky mumbles, and you're sucked in to his fever dream. Twenty years on, it's still acutely pertinent to ethnic minority experience in what was once called 'the mother country'.

Debate continues today about whether Hayes himself may have been influenced, consciously or not, on 'Ike's Rap II' by the hippie Belgian band the Wallace Collection's 1969 reverie 'Daydream'. It's difficult to prove. Some melodies are just in the ether. In 2015 'Ike's Rap II' resurfaced again, with Hayes's vocal haunting the background, on the Canadian Alessia Cara's

debut single 'Here'. The then 18-year-old Cara does a decent job as a trainee Amy Winehouse, although she was the first to credit her producers, Pop & Oak, for adding the Hayes loop. Prior to that, it was squeezed thin and submerged by the London rapper Maverick Sabre in his 2011 song 'Let Me Go'.

South Park, and particularly his complicity in the self-parodic 'Chocolate Salty Balls' song, has made Hayes, who died in 2008 aged 65, a figure of fun for many people. Yet he deserves to be remembered as an artist of huge originality and reach, who spawned work – both his own and that of the brilliant Bristolians – of enduring urgency and passion.

Richard Clayton

46

I BELIEVE IN FATHER CHRISTMAS

It's warm, catchy as hell, one of the most enduringly popular Christmas songs, and yet its roots lie in that thoroughly un-poppy genre, prog rock. 'I Believe in Father Christmas' was written by Greg Lake, who died in December 2016 at the age of 69, and Pete Sinfield; Lake was bassist and singer with the hyper-technical trio Emerson, Lake & Palmer, while he and Sinfield had previously been members of prog pioneers King Crimson (Sinfield it was who wrote '21st Century Schizoid Man' with its apocalyptic couplets such as 'Cat's foot, iron claw/ Neuro-surgeons scream for more').

ELP's keyboardist Keith Emerson had encouraged each member of the band to come up with solo material, so in 1975 Lake teamed up with lyricist Sinfield to create something out of a 'Christmassy' chord sequence Lake had written. The result was thoughtful, but melodic too: a humanist, anti-consumerist Christmas song that also manages to warm the cockles. And by adding a snippet of twinkling sleigh-ride music by Sergei Prokofiev, they summoned the sparkle of Christmas, creating, as Sinfield has said, 'a picture-postcard Christmas, with morbid edges'.

The lyrics are mostly Sinfield's, and the first two verses juxta-pose his own early memories of Christmas ('eyes full of tinsel and fire') with his subsequent loss of innocence ('And I saw him and through his disguise'). At this point Sinfield was concerned that the song would be too bleak, so he resolved matters with a more uplifting final verse ('I wish you a hopeful Christmas').

Meanwhile, Emerson – whose love of classical music had led ELP into crossover adventures in their Moog-driven arrangements of pieces such as Mussorgsky's *Pictures at an Exhibition* – suggested inserting the Prokofiev snippet. This section of the story is worthy of a *Life of a Song* of its own. At the time he wrote it, Prokofiev was living in Paris, pining for his homeland, a former proponent of dissonance who had steadily turned to composing the more melodic material favoured by his Soviet paymasters before his eventual return to Moscow in 1936.

In 1933, Prokofiev was commissioned to write the score for the satirical film *Lieutenant Kijé*, and the resulting composition was well received. These were early days for film composers, and the jaunty 'Troika' section eventually used by Lake was one of the first pieces of film music to become an orchestral suite. In the film itself, the troika sequence features not, as might be imagined, a magical three-horse sleigh journey through glistening snowscapes, but a drunken night-time trip in which one of the characters is so addled by drink that he tumbles off the sleigh. The melody is initially sung; Prokofiev's tune comes from an old Hussar drinking song which runs, dissolutely: 'Like a roadside inn is a woman's heart, where travellers stop and stay; checking in or checking out, all the night and all the day.'

'I Believe in Father Christmas' was a hit worldwide, kept from the UK Number 1 slot only by Queen's gargantuan smash 'Bohemian Rhapsody'. It has subsequently become a perennial on radio playlists and, ironically, given its anti-commercial lyrics ('They sold me a dream of Christmas'), supermarket soundtracks. The promotional film for the single was a curious affair, shot partly in the caves where the Dead Sea Scrolls were discovered.

Lake re-recorded the song several times with his ELP colleagues and with orchestras, but the original, with its resonant acoustic guitar, remains the best. Cover versions range from the excruciating (2009 *X Factor* winner Joe McElderry's version has a jaunty beat that's wildly inappropriate) to the bombastic (U2's Bono batters listeners into submission when he goes up an octave). Susan Boyle's version has a Caledonian lilt. The British band Embrace strip it back to piano and voice, and the result is touching.

Also worth mentioning in dispatches is a rendition, available on YouTube, featuring Lake alongside fellow prog-rock veteran Ian Anderson of Jethro Tull, on flute. They were performing in St Bride's Church in London in 2006, and the recording is not of the highest quality, but with Anderson's delicate flute ornamentations, and bolstered by the church organ, the song's spirit shines through.

David Cheal

SUKIYAKI

In June 1963, a Japanese pop song soared to the top of the American Billboard Hot 100 chart. More than 50 years later, 'Sukiyaki' remains the only Japanese song to have done so. Ironic, when you learn that lyricist Rokusuke Ei wrote it partly as a lament over the Japanese government's capitulation to a treaty extending the status of American bases in Japan.

Born in 1933 and raised in the grounds of Buddhist temple, Ei was evacuated to the countryside during the war, which informed a passionate, life-long support of pacifism. A popular radio personality right until his death in 2016 at the age of 83, Ei defended the military-renouncing Article 9 of the post-war constitution, and condemned a recent campaign to revise it.

In the late 1950s he teamed up with piano prodigy Hachidai Nakamura, who had been turned on to jazz by American military radio. Both young men were part of a new generation bored by the sentimental and formulaic 'mudo kayo' songs popular with those drowning their post-war sorrows in Japan's blue-collar bars. Nakamura wrote light, free, danceable melodies and Ei used vernacular lyrics: together they revolutionized Japanese pop.

Despite Ei's commitment to leftist causes, their catchy hits were part of a fluffy, escapist cultural movement targeted at the new, aspirational urban middle classes. Translating roughly as 'I look up as I walk', 'Ue o Muite Aruko' reflects Ei's determination to remain optimistic for his newborn son in the face of political events that included the treaty with the US, the death of a student on a protest march and the assassination of a socialist leader live on TV by a samurai sword-wielding rightwing teenager.

When the song was premiered live in August 1961, Ei was upset that 19-year-old rockabilly singer Kyu Sakamoto bopped so glibly through his profound expressions of 'hitoribocchi' (loneliness). But the song was an instant earworm. British record executive Louis Benjamin snapped it up for jazzman Kenny Ball's Dixieland band while on a visit to Tokyo in 1962. Suspecting that the original title was too difficult for Western audiences, Benjamin rechristened it, somewhat disrespectfully, after his favourite Japanese beef stew: 'Sukiyaki'.

Soon American DJs caught on to the original record and Sakamoto's version became an international bestseller (though it kept its title, 'Sukiyaki'). Writing for the BBC on the song's 50th anniversary, American John Taylor said its popularity marked a turning point as his countrymen 'began to see Japanese people not just as a former enemy or some mysterious, exotic race, but as people with feelings no different from their own, and capable of expressing beautiful, tender emotions'.

Covers soon blossomed in many languages. 1963 welcomed a Portuguese version by Brazil's Trio Esperança, and Indo-Dutch duo The Blue Diamonds sang it in German. Soul man Jewel Akens wrote the first English lyrics on his brassy 'My First Lonely Night' (1966).

The best-known English lyrics were written by Californian disco duo A Taste of Honey, who turned it into a break-up ballad in 1980. The duo's singer Janice-Marie Johnson was heartbroken herself when she recorded it and credits 'Sukiyaki' with 'teaching me you can't cry and sing at the same time'.

It was A Taste of Honey's version that infiltrated early hip-hop, sung by London-born Slick Rick (on 1985's dexterous, misogynist 'La Di Da Di') and Snoop Dogg on his 1993 tribute 'Lodi Dodi'.

In 2015 *X Factor* runner-up Olly Murs gave it a nasal, noughties spin as 'I Look at the Sky', complete with whistling and fresh lyrics by Yoko Ono.

The most poignant recent rendition came from British-born violinist Diana Yukawa, whose father was killed (before she was born) in a plane crash in 1985. In 2000, aged just 15, she played it on the mountain where Japan Airlines Flight 123 hit the ground after 32 minutes of worsening technical failures during which some passengers had time to scribble final words to their loved ones. Five hundred and twenty people were killed; also among the dead was the song's original singer, Sakamoto.

Helen Brown

48

ME AND
BOBBY MCGEE

Few artists embodied the 1960s counter-culture as fully or as fatally as Janis Joplin. A self-described Texan 'misfit', she outrageously lived – and died – the rock 'n' roll life, blasting the Monterey Pop festival with her volcanic eruption of a blues voice, dressing in tripped-out granny chic and commissioning the cult cartoonist Robert Crumb to create an album sleeve. A heroin overdose killed her in October 1970, but the following January one of her last recorded songs became a Number 1 single in the US. Joplin's telling of 'Me and Bobby McGee' would be her epitaph; its vocal shot through with all her 'hurts and confusions' yet also her immense vitality and rowdy romantic vigour.

Joplin's version might be definitive – it's easy to imagine her travelling every mile of the lovers' journey from Kentucky to California – but she didn't write 'Me and Bobby McGee', nor was hers the earliest cover. Kris Kristofferson, an old flame, was the author, although he didn't write it for her either, and his song proved an instant country classic. A former army captain and Rhodes Scholar, Kristofferson would become a successful actor and singer, but in the late 1960s he was jobbing as a studio gopher in Nashville as he tried to make it as a songwriter.

'Me and Bobby McGee' was his breakthrough, but it wasn't entirely his idea. Fred Foster, the boss of Monument Records, challenged Kristofferson to write a song with the title 'Me and Bobby McKee', about a pair of drifters, with the twist being that Bobby was a girl. Bobby McKee was a secretary in Foster's building. Kristofferson misheard her name as 'McGee', but took on the assignment. He had been hanging out with a fellow Texan musician, Mickey Newbury, and it was the metre of Newbury's 'Why You Been Gone So Long?' that guided Kristofferson's melody. Kristofferson's most quotable line – 'Freedom's just another word for nothing left to lose' – was inspired, he later said, by a scene in Fellini's film *La Strada*, in which Anthony Quinn leaves Giulietta Masina and comes to regret it.

'Me and Bobby McGee' was picked up by the 'King of the Road' singer Roger Miller. His original recording, with boxy drumming and an almost mariachi flourish at the end, became a hit in 1969. Miller, too, was from Texas. 'Me and Bobby McGee' had many of the characteristics of the musical style attributed to that state called 'outlaw country': rootsy yet wordy, gritty and reflective, unafraid to cross the borders into folk and blues.

The song's subsequent recording history is a *Who's Who* of that renegade genre, with versions from Charlie McCoy to Johnny Cash and Waylon Jennings to Chet Atkins, as well as delightful performances by female stars such as Dottie West and Loretta Lynn. The hippies' favourite jam band, the Grateful Dead, turned it into a platform for Jerry Garcia's rueful guitar soloing on the 1971 live album known as *Skull & Roses*. Kristofferson's own elegiac rendition was released on his debut album of April 1970.

But two other versions of that era were soon better known: Gordon Lightfoot's solemn acoustic take and the up-tempo country pop of Kenny Rogers & The First Edition. More recently, Melissa Etheridge, LeAnn Rimes and Pink are among those influenced by Joplin's *con belto* approach (without ever really coming close). In 2002, the actress and singer Jennifer Love Hewitt bizarrely did it with bongos. There have also been covers in Swedish, German and Italian – the latter Gianna Nannini's funky little noodle in 1979.

Kristofferson heard Joplin's account the night after her death. It broke him up. Yet interest in his work soared after her posthumous Number 1. Kristofferson surely kept such success in perspective. 'Me and Bobby McGee' is about loving and losing. 'Feelin' good was good enough for me – and Janis,' he ad-libbed in a concert in 2010. I reckon he meant it.

Richard Clayton

49

MY FUNNY VALENTINE

The 1937 Rodgers and Hart musical *Babes in Arms*, which gave generations of grateful cabaret singers 'My Funny Valentine', also virtually invented the 'Hey, let's put on a show!' genre. They did childcare differently in those days – in the musical, a group of home-alone teens must do something useful with their time to stop the local sheriff carrying out his threat to send them to the work farm. This is the Great Depression, and the parents are off working the vaudeville circuit.

The plot was flimsy and later much parodied, but the show produced several classic hits: 'The Lady Is a Tramp', 'Where or When' and 'I Wish I Were in Love Again'. 'My Funny Valentine' became such a ubiquitous torch song over the years that, as the writer Alec Wilder noted in *American Popular Song* (1972), the owner of one New York club 'inserted in all contracts with vocalists a clause which stated they were forbidden to sing it'.

The original Rodgers and Hart number was sung by a female lead, fondly listing the faults of the lead male, Valentine LaMar. 'Is your figure less than Greek?/Is your mouth a little weak?/ When you open it to speak, are you smart?' But deeper feelings are revealed when the rhythm kicks in and she sings the refrain: 'You're my funny Valentine, sweet comic Valentine/You make me smile with my heart'. A *Variety* reviewer worried that 'no nudity, no show girls, no plush or gold plate may mean no sale', but the 1937 Broadway show stretched to 289 performances.

In 1939 Busby Berkeley directed a film version of *Babes in Arms* starring Judy Garland and Mickey Rooney. However, both plot and songs were drastically altered; 'My Funny Valentine' was one of nearly a dozen numbers set adrift. It resurfaced in the 1957 Frank Sinatra and Rita Hayworth vehicle *Pal Joey*, lip-synced by Kim Novak in a nightclub setting, imbuing the song with the bittersweet hints of doomed romance that were to remain its stock-in-trade.

Meanwhile, the composition made slow but steady inroads into the jazz repertoire. The song charted briefly with a sweet-toned big-band version recorded by the Hal McIntyre Orchestra in 1944. As became the norm, the introductory verse was removed and the band cut straight to the bittersweet refrain. Baritone saxophonist Gerry Mulligan picked it up for his Quartet in 1952 and the austere, piano-free reading was the perfect vehicle for Chet Baker's trumpet.

Among the many instrumental versions around, pianist Bill Evans and guitarist Jim Hall's up-tempo duet on the 1962 album *Undercurrent* stands out. In 1954, Sinatra included it on *Songs for Young Lovers*, his first collaboration with bandleader Nelson Riddle. Baker recorded the tune again – this time as a vocalist – on his 1956 hit album *Chet Baker Sings*, and revisited it many times over the years, especially in live performance.

The song had gone mainstream, and the consensus on how many artists recorded it stands at about 600. Ella Fitzgerald recorded the song in its entirety – a rare thing – in a pristine 1957 cover featuring the Buddy Bregman Orchestra. Miles Davis also made the song part of his repertoire and recorded

it several times. The best is a live 1964 concert recording of a fundraising benefit for black voter registration in Mississippi. It is a 15-minute, shape-shifting, mood-changing masterpiece.

A *Babes in Arms* subplot concerned a wealthy southerner bankrolling the show on the proviso that two African–American kids were sacked from the cast. So it's pleasing to note that a Chaka Khan account of 'My Funny Valentine' was part of the award-winning soundtrack of the 1995 Whitney Houston movie *Waiting to Exhale*, which featured an all African–American cast.

But it is with Baker that the song has come to be most identified. In a nightclub scene in the 1999 film *The Talented Mr Ripley*, Matt Damon's Ripley performs a version, closely emulating Chet Baker's singing style to conjure a tangible sense of the late 1950s. A song that started life in a Depression-era musical comedy ended up associated with the boom years and a musician, Baker, whose life ended in tragedy.

Mike Hobart

50

AULD LANG SYNE

In the closing scene of the 1989 romcom *When Harry Met Sally*, the titular friends-turned-lovers have kissed at a New Year's party. 'Auld Lang Syne' is playing. Harry (Billy Crystal) is struck by a thought. 'What does this song mean? My whole life, I don't know what this song means. I mean, "Should old acquaintance be forgot"? Does that mean we should forget old acquaintances, or does it mean if we happen to forget them, we should remember them, which is not possible because we already forgot them?' Sally, played by Meg Ryan, responds: 'Well, maybe it just means that we should remember that we forgot them or something. Anyway, it's about old friends.'

Sally has hit the nail on the head: the title of this sentimental air translates from lowland Scots as 'old long since', and it's about reunions as much as separations. But where did it spring from? In the latter years of his life the poet Robert Burns became an avid collector of Scottish folk songs and ballads and, having heard 'Auld Lang Syne' from 'an old man' in 1788, he transcribed and embellished this 'exceedingly expressive' lowland song.

Burns sent the lyric to two publishers. The first was James Johnson, who included it in a collection called *The Scots Musical Museum* (1796); in this version, it was set to an old Scottish melody that Burns himself did not much care for. The second was George Thomson, who published it in *A Select Collection of Original Scottish Airs* in 1799, three years after Burns' death. It was set to a tune known as 'Sir Alexander Don's Strathspey' (a *strathspey* being a type of dance), and it's this tune that is widely sung today.

The song quickly became popular at Hogmanay gatherings, and as the Scots diaspora scattered around the globe, the song travelled with them. (In today's parlance, it went viral.) In the 1914 Christmas truce, British and German troops emerged from their trenches to play football and sing 'Auld Lang Syne'. The song has also become hugely popular in Southeast Asia. And many Japanese department stores play 'Auld Lang Syne' over the PA system to signify that they are closing. International scout jamborees often close with it.

Even before the arrival of the talkies, Hollywood had cottoned on to the song's potency, often using it to highlight unhappiness through juxtaposition. In Charlie Chaplin's 1925 silent weepie *The Gold Rush*, revellers in a saloon bar link hands to sing 'Auld Lang Syne' while Chaplin's character mopes in his cabin. It features in the tearful climax to *It's a Wonderful Life* (1946). Billy Wilder's 1960 classic *The Apartment* ends with Shirley MacLaine, miserable at a New Year's party with the dreadful Mr Sheldrake as the band play 'Auld Lang Syne', before she takes her leave and ends up playing cards with Jack Lemmon. And while it may seem sacrilege to mention 2008's *Sex and the City* movie in the same paragraph as these classics, that film does feature a moving New Year montage with 'Auld Lang Syne' in its original melody, beautifully sung by Mairi Campbell.

As for recorded versions: it was first committed to gramophone disc in 1890 by Emile Berliner, the inventor of the medium (through the crackles he can be heard making the common mistake of pronouncing 'syne' as 'zyne'). Elvis, Hendrix and Springsteen have covered it. It is perhaps best to draw a veil over the 1976 disco version by the Salsoul Orchestra, and Cliff Richard's exquisitely awful millennium mash-up with 'The Lord's Prayer' as a lyric, and celebrate instead its appearance on a 2011 song called 'New Year's Eve'. This wonderfully woozy, boozy ballad twice breaks into 'Auld Lang Syne'. The singer? There can surely be no voice better suited to the song's slurring, small-hours sentimentality than that of Tom Waits.

David Cheal

INDEX

PHOTO CREDITS

19 Lee Hazlewood and Nancy Sinatra recording in the studio, *c*.1966; © Michael Ochs Archives/Getty Images

20 Leonard Cohen, mid 1980s; © Oliver Morris/Getty Images

21 Aretha Franklin rehearsing, *c*.1972; © Michael Ochs Archives/Getty Images

23 Marvin Gaye 1964; © Pictorial Press Ltd / Alamy Stock Photo

24 Glen Campbell, 1967; © Donaldson Collection/Michael Ochs Archives/Getty Images

25 Britney Spears, 2003; © Jeff Kravitz/FilmMagic/Getty Images

26 Ian Gillan, lead singer with Deep Purple, performing in Copenhagen, 1972; © Jan Persson/Redferns/Getty Images

28 Elvis Costello performing in New York, 1982; © Michael Putland/Getty Images

29 Ike Turner's band Kings of Rhythm (back row left to right) Jackie Brenston, Raymond Hill, Eddie Jones, Fred Sample and Billy Gayles (front row left to right) Jesse Knight Jr., Ike Turner and Eugene Washington, 1956; © King Collection/Photoshot/Getty Images

32 Sam Cooke, *c*.1960; © Jess Rand/Michael Ochs Archives/Getty Images

34 Bruce Springsteen during his *Born in the USA* tour, 1984–5; © Ebet Roberts/Redferns/Getty Images

36 Judy Garland in *The Wizard of Oz*, 1939; © Metro-Goldwyn-Mayer/MGM Studios/Moviepix/Getty Images

37 Kirk Hammett of Metallica, 1991; © Mick Hutson/Redferns/Getty Images

40 Woody Guthrie, *c*.1943; © Donaldson Collection/Michael Ochs Archives/ Library of Congress/Getty Images

41 Patti Smith performing in Central Park, New York, 1978; © Richard E. Aaron/Redferns/Getty Images

42 Julie Andrews in *The Sound of Music*, 1965; © 20th Century Fox/Kobal/REX/Shutterstock

43 Randy Newman; © Alan Messer/Rex/Shutterstock

44 Christine McVie and Stevie Nicks of Fleetwood Mac, performing at the Omni Coliseum, Atlanta, 1977; © Rick Diamond/Getty Images

45 Isaac Hayes photographed for *GQ* magazine, 1971; © Peter Hujar/Condé Nast via Getty Images

48 Janis Joplin, *c.*1970; © Michael Ochs Archives/Getty Images

49 Chaka Khan performing in Berlin, 1995; © Baltzer/ullstein bild via Getty Images